CHOSEN
IN CHRIST

CHOSEN
IN CHRIST

THE GLORY OF GRACE
IN EPHESIANS 1

RICHARD D. PHILLIPS

P U B L I S H I N G
P.O. BOX 817 • PHILLIPSBURG • NEW JERSEY 08865-0817

Page design by Lakeside Design Plus
Typesetting by Michelle Feaster

Printed in the United States of America

Library of Congress Cataloging-in-Publication Data

Phillips, Richard D. (Richard Davis), 1960–
       Chosen in Christ : the glory of grace in Ephesians 1 / Richard D. Phillips.
              p. cm.
       Includes bibliographical references and index.
       ISBN 0-87552-792-2
       1. Bible. N.T. Ephesians I—Commentaries. I. Title.

BS2695.53.P48 2004
227'.5077—dc22

                                        2003066363

To

CARLYLE (BUD) WILSON
with gratitude for fatherly love,
for brotherly prayers, and for a passion
to see a modern reformation in Christ's church

Ephesians 5:1–2

and to

HIM
in whom we are blessed with
every spiritual blessing in heavenly
places, blessed be his God and Father!

Ephesians 1:3

CONTENTS

PREFACE

There is no greater need today than for people to understand and believe and act upon the message that is found in the apostle Paul's great letter to the Ephesians. Here we are presented with the triune God in all his glory, but especially in his work for the salvation of lost humankind. Ephesians contains the Christian gospel in full orb, saving us from our sin and transforming us into the image of God's holy Son. Anyone who grasps the message of this book will apprehend the Bible's essential teaching on salvation, on the church, and on the Christian life. All Scripture is of course edifying and instructive, but here we climb to the peak of apostolic teaching, the top of the pyramid in which all the main lines come together.

In the preface to his volume on Ephesians 1, written in 1978, D. Martyn Lloyd-Jones declared, "Our world is in a state of utter confusion, and, alas, the same is true of the Christian Church and of many individual Christians."[1] How alarming that is to read, since our generation looks back on that time with nostalgia as one of ordered simplicity and comparative virtue! I know of no one who would argue that the world, and Christians with it, is less confused now than then; in the intervening years Western civilization has plunged headlong into a sinful descent, so that confusion not only reigns but is widely celebrated. To the Christian, what is most alarming is the extent to which what is said of the world can be said of the church and of professing Christian people. The most urgent need of our time, then, as Lloyd-Jones argued in his, is for us to learn anew what the word *Christian* means. This is the particular subject that the apostle Paul treats with such clarity and richness in the first chapter of Ephesians. In so doing, he not only scatters the clouds of confusion but also shatters them with the light of God's magnificent grace in Christ, inspiring us to live in gratitude to the pleasure and praise of God.

In my view, Lloyd-Jones's expositions on Ephesians set the standard for studies of this great epistle. However, many pastors and laypeople will find his commentary—at eight volumes, each of them quite long—sufficiently daunting so as to let them fall into neglect. My experience is that most of the other resources on Ephesians suffer for being too short. As Lloyd-Jones lamented, briefer treatments want for a thorough consideration of the details, passing by diamonds and gems laid with such care into this, the crown of the great apostle's written achievement. My intention is to strike the wide-open middle ground of this situation, offering a thorough yet accessible exposition of Ephesians to the reader interested in really coming to grips with this most elevated and instructive book of Holy Scripture.

The studies in this volume were first preached at Tenth Presbyterian Church in Philadelphia from the fall of 2001 to the spring of 2002, as part of a series on the entire Book of Ephesians. I will always be grateful to the session and congregation of Tenth Church for the love and encouragement they provided me during my time of ministry there. I also thank the session and congregation of First Presbyterian Church in Coral Springs/Margate, Florida, where I now serve as senior minister, for their constant love and prayers.

This book is dedicated to Bud Wilson, a man whose life exemplifies the faith and love Paul wants all Christians to offer to God. I am particularly indebted to him for his fervent and loving support of my ministry, in prayer and in deed. I am again indebted to my friend Bruce Bell for his invaluable aid in critiquing these chapters. I give praise to God for the faithful support of my wife, Sharon, without which my ministry would lack endurance and joy. Finally, I give thanks to the God and Father of our Lord Jesus Christ for the superabundance of spiritual blessings he so graciously gives to sinners, "to the praise of his glorious grace."

1

GRACE AND PEACE TO YOU

Ephesians 1:1–2

Paul, an apostle of Christ Jesus by the will of God,
To the saints who are in Ephesus, and are faithful
in Christ Jesus: Grace to you and peace from
God our Father and the Lord Jesus Christ.
—Ephesians 1:1–2

aul's Epistle to the Ephesians has been celebrated with the highest possible superlatives. Samuel Taylor Coleridge called it "the divinest composition of man."[1] It has likewise been described as "the crown of St. Paul's writings" and "the Queen of the Epistles." John Mackay, former president of Princeton Theological Seminary, described Ephesians as the "greatest," the "maturest," and "for our time the most relevant of all Paul's works. For here is the distilled essence of the Christian religion, the most authoritative and most consummate compendium of our holy Christian faith." Recounting his own conversion through the reading of this letter, Mackay describes his experience: "I saw a new world . . . everything was new . . . I had a new outlook, new experiences, new attitudes to other people. I loved God. Jesus Christ became the center of everything . . . I had been 'quickened'; I was really alive."[2] This aptly describes what Ephesians is all about.

Realizing the profundity of this book may lead some readers to apprehension. In one sense that is all right; we should begin studies of a book of Scripture—especially one described like this—with awe, with a sense that something is going to happen to us through our study. It is the Paul's intention that this should be so, and God's intention through him! But to temper that apprehension, we should realize that though Ephesians is so profound, it is marked by a simple clarity. James Montgomery Boice wrote, when he began preaching this book, "If Ephesians *is* profound, it is so not for the mysterious nature of its unfathomable deep secrets, but for the clear way it presents the most basic Christian truths. . . . What is the appeal of this book? In my judgment it is just this: it presents the basic doctrines of Christianity comprehensively, clearly, practically, and winsomely."[3]

PAUL, AN APOSTLE

Following the custom of his day, Paul began this letter with his name and office: "Paul, an apostle of Christ Jesus." Paul wrote thirteen biblical books, just under one quarter of the New Testament. Apart from Jesus Christ, it is hard to think of anyone who left so great a mark on the history of the Christian church.

F. F. Bruce began his study of Paul's life by frankly admitting his love for the great apostle. He praised Paul for "the attractive warmth of his personality, his intellectual stature, the exhilarating release effected by his gospel of redeeming grace, the dynamism with which he propagated that gospel throughout the world."[4] Paul is best known for the depth and coherence of his theological writings, but as Thomas Schreiner reminds us in a recent study, "Paul . . . was first and foremost a missionary . . . who wrote letters to churches in order to sustain his converts in their newfound faith."[5]

Paul describes himself more simply and quite a bit more humbly than all that: "Paul, an apostle of Christ Jesus." The word *apostle* means "one who is sent," or simply, "messenger." In the New Testament era apostles were missionaries who traveled about preaching the gospel and forming churches. Most importantly—and surely this sense is intended by Paul—apostles bore the authority of Christ in their teaching and rule, an authority granted them by the risen and exalted Lord Jesus. D. Martyn Lloyd-Jones defines an apostle as "one chosen and sent with a special mission as the fully authorized representative of the sender."[6] P. T. O'Brien writes, "As an apostle he has the authority to proclaim the gospel in both oral and written form, as well as to establish and build up churches."[7]

The apostles include the original twelve disciples of Jesus, with Matthias added to replace the betrayer Judas Iscariot. Acts 1:22 establishes the qualification that an apostle must be a witness of the resurrection of Jesus Christ. Paul fulfilled this criterion by means of his conversion experience on the Damascus Road, when he was converted and commissioned by the risen Lord. Paul was not one of the original apostles, but in Galatians 2:1–10 he recounts being received by them after his conversion and accepted by them as an apostle appointed to preach to the Gentiles.

Paul asserts his apostolic authority in all of his writings, presenting his credentials and drawing attention to the official character of his writing. What Jesus said to the Twelve just before his ascension into heaven, in Acts 1:8, equally applies to Paul, "You will receive power . . . you will be my witnesses." The Christian faith, therefore, is received through the apostolic testimony, which is the exalted Christ's revelation by the inspiration of the Holy Spirit through these delegates. We, like the first recipients, are bound to receive and believe the words of these apostles as the very Word of Christ.

Paul adds that he is an apostle of Christ "by the will of God." This was not a job Paul had sought and worked toward on his own. He was called by God and equipped by God's grace. It is on this basis that his teaching is to be received: not because of his own native genius and persuasive power but in submission to God, who appointed him. It is this contrast between divine and human authority that Paul probably means to emphasize here; the opening words of Galatians work this out even more clearly: "Paul, an apostle—not from men nor through man, but through Jesus Christ and God the Father" (Gal. 1:1).

This is the first of four times in Ephesians 1 that Paul speaks of "the will of God." This directs us right from the start to one of the great themes that runs all through this epistle, namely, the sovereignty of God. The other verses in which this expression appears—Ephesians 1:5, 9, and 11—emphasize God's sovereignty in our salvation and his eternal purpose to bring all things together under Jesus Christ. This is an important connection, because it tells us that from start to finish the gospel and Christianity are under the sovereign control of God. God sovereignly accomplished our redemption through Jesus Christ; by his own will he sent apostles to preach the gospel of Christ; he sovereignly chose us from before creation to receive that gospel and be saved; and at the time of his choosing he will sovereignly consummate and complete his redemptive plan in Christ to the glory of his name. It is all a matter of God's sovereignty; we encounter this in the first verse of the book, just as we will find it standing out in glory all through Ephesians.

AUTHORSHIP AND DESTINATION

Scholars have posed two questions that are important to our study of Ephesians. The first has to do with whether or not Paul wrote the letter. It is surprising to find that the majority of biblical scholars today deny its Pauline authorship, most of them arguing that some brilliant assistant wrote Ephesians many years after Paul died, using his name for credibility.

Those who argue this way point out the impersonal character of Ephesians, which seems odd if Paul were writing to a church where he had preached for two and a half years. But this is explained when we realize that Ephesians seems to have been written as a theological tract for wider circulation. Additionally, scholars cite a significant difference in language and style between Ephesians and other known Pauline letters. Forty-one words appear only here, and eighty-four more are found in the New Testament but not elsewhere in Paul's letters. But other letters also have a distinctive style and vocabulary, and, as William Barclay observes, "It would be ridiculous to demand that a man with a mind like Paul's should never add to his vocabulary and should always express himself in the same way."[8] Another argument is the similarity between Colossians and Ephesians; the theory is advanced that the writer of Ephesians used this other Pauline letter as his model. But it is hard to see how this similarity argues against rather than for Paul as the author of Ephesians.

Most importantly, this letter in God's Word explicitly claims to come from the apostle Paul. For another writer to have used his name involves fraud, especially since he asks for the readers to pray for his—Paul's—ministry. Such a situation is inconceivable within a biblical view of the divine inspiration of Scripture, and as Charles Hodge observed, Ephesians "reveals itself as the work of the Holy Ghost as clearly as the stars declare their maker to be God."[9] As for the legitimacy of pseudonymous writings, the early church vigorously excluded such frauds from the canon, punishing those who attempted to pass off their own writings as apostolic. The early church universally accepted Ephesians as Pauline, and objections to the contrary speak more eloquently against the state of scholarship today than they do about the authorship of this great letter.[10]

The second issue has to do with the recipients of the letter. The problem is that the best early manuscripts do not contain the words "in Ephesus" in Ephesians 1:1. This, combined with the impersonal style of the letter, strongly argues that Paul did not write this letter specifically to the church in Ephesus. I think the best explanation—though by no means certain— is that Paul wrote Ephesians as a circular letter or tract, which he sent with Colossians for the general benefit of the churches in western Asia Minor. Ephesians 6:21 says that a man named Tychicus would update the readers on Paul's situation; Colossians 4:8 tells us that the same Tychicus was bearing that letter. It seems that Paul learned of the heresy in Colosse and wrote Colossians in response. Since his messenger would travel through Ephesus and up the Lycus Valley, Paul wrote Ephesians as well, which was intended for the building up of the churches along the way. This also explains the similarity between Ephesians and Colossians. Some scholars suggest that Ephesians is really the missing letter to Laodicea mentioned in Colossians 4:16, but in that case it is hard to see how later manuscripts incorporated the words "to . . . Ephesus" and why there are no copies listing Laodicea as the recipient of what we know as Ephesians.

Obviously, some mystery remains, but we can be sure that Paul the apostle wrote Ephesians along with Colossians for the benefit of churches in the vicinity of Ephesus in western Asia Minor, probably in the early A.D. 60s, during his first imprisonment at Rome.

PEACE WITH GOD

Paul concludes his salutation with words found at the beginning of almost all of his letters: "Grace to you and peace from God our Father and the Lord Jesus Christ." Paul always interjects theology into his greetings, and here at the outset he puts before us the two great themes of this letter: grace and peace. Ephesians 1–3 commends to us the grace of God in all its greatness, while Ephesians 4–6 calls us to the life of peace. The two are woven together all through Ephesians, the great message of which is the bringing together of all things in Christ by means of God's grace and with the effect of peace through all God's creation. Lloyd-Jones sums up this relationship between grace and peace: "Grace is the beginning of our faith; peace is the end of our faith. Grace is the fountain, the spring, the source. . . . But what does the Christian life mean, what is it meant to produce? The answer is 'peace.'"[11]

Before looking at the meaning and theological significance of grace, let us first consider the peace that comes from God and the Lord Jesus Christ. The first thing we need to understand is what the Bible means by peace and how the word is normally used today. For us, peace is the absence of strife, of war, of conflict. We sign peace treaties, and the only effect is that the actual fighting comes to a halt. The hatred is still there, the causes of strife are unrelieved, no sense of unity arises and certainly no love. Yet we celebrate such things as peace. The same is true in our workplaces and families. But the Bible always ridicules such an idea of peace. The prophet cried, "'Peace, peace,' they say, 'when there is no peace'" (Jer. 6:14 NIV).

7

The biblical idea of peace is very different. Here, the idea is mainly positive: It is *shalom,* the blessedness of peace and harmony. Leon Morris comments, "Paul . . . is not saying here that he trusts that the Ephesian believers will not find themselves caught up in a war. He is speaking about the deep and abiding peace that comes when people are right with God."[12] R. C. Sproul expressed the contrast by referring to the attempts to avert World War II. He remarks, "There is a vast difference between Neville Chamberlain's leaning over a balcony declaring, 'We have achieved peace in our time' and Jesus' leaning over a table to say, 'Peace I leave with you, My peace I give unto you; not as the world gives do I give to you' (Jn. 14:27)."[13]

Peace is the great need of humankind. Our great problem is that there is no peace because of sin. First of all this pertains to our relationship with God. There is peace neither between man and God nor between God and man. Paul writes in Romans 8:7 that "the sinful mind is hostile to God. It does not submit to God's law, nor can it do so" (NIV). Paul begins Ephesians 2 by expounding this in detail, speaking of people's transgressions and sins, their disobedience and their loyalty to a kingdom that is hostile to God's kingdom. Lloyd-Jones explains, "Man by nature, as he is born into this world, is a hater of God. . . . He fights God, he is an enemy . . . everything in him by nature is utterly opposed to God."[14] That is the teaching of Ephesians. People will deny this; perhaps you do. But let me then ask you to submit your life to God, to give God the worship he is due, to serve his kingdom, to repent of your sins and let him tell you what to do, to let his law tell you what is right and wrong, to trust and love and follow God. We will find all too clearly that what the Bible says, is right. In your own strength, according to your sinful nature, you cannot and will not do it. Humankind is at war with God.

The inevitable result is that God is alienated from us in return. Paul begins his doctrinal section of Romans by saying,

"The wrath of God is revealed from heaven against all un-godliness and unrighteousness of men" (Rom. 1:18). In Ephesians 2:3 Paul says that people, because of their sinful nature, are objects of God's wrath. The peace of the gospel, then, is one that reconciles us to God through Jesus Christ. This is the great problem of the world—humanity is at enmity with God and under his wrath in return—and here is the great solution, one that not only solves the problem but also brings such great positive benefit—peace with God and peace from God. This peace comes only through faith in the Lord Jesus Christ.

The bulk of Ephesians 1 is given to praise of God for his many blessings of peace. First, he solves the problem and removes the barrier. The problem is sin; the answer is Christ the Redeemer, the only answer to the great problem of our alienation with God. He offered his blood to gain our forgiveness, dying in our place upon the cross. Here, too, we see the positive aspects of peace with God—not just the removal of conflict, not just a piece of paper saying there will be no fighting for a while. God's peace means fellowship, unity, love. Ephesians 1:5 says that God adopted us as his children through Jesus Christ. This is peace—a right and loving relationship with God. Notice how Paul puts it in Ephesians 1:2; it is peace from God as our Father and Jesus Christ as our Lord. That is the relationship of peace that Paul wishes us through his gospel message, that we may be brought into God's family with him as our Father and then have power to live with him in peace under the lordship of Jesus Christ.

All of this is through the death and resurrection of Jesus Christ; Paul's gospel is centered on the person and work of Jesus. As he says in Ephesians 2:14, "He himself is our peace." Do you know peace with God? Are you able to say you have his favor, his love? Do you love him in return, longing to do his will, to know him? The only way you can is by coming to God through faith in Christ, confessing your sin and enmity to God

9

and trusting Christ's life and death and resurrection, all of which were given for you to be reconciled to God.

PEACE ON EARTH

But Paul's vision is not limited to peace between heaven and earth; he also sees peace reigning in the place of the turmoil of this world. What about peace among the nations—isn't this the very thing our age is clamoring for? Look back over the last century, and what progress have we really made? We have gone several decades without a world war, yet the world has been in constant strife all the same. Look at the hatred, the bombings, the violence—not just in the Middle East but also in Africa, in Europe, in our own cities. There is no peace upon the earth, and human attempts to produce it have been shown for their futility. Think, too, about our relationships, our families, our workplaces, our neighborhoods. Is there not division of every kind: racial, economic, ethnic, regional, and professional strife?

What is the answer? The answer is not training, not compulsion, not treaties; the problem is simply too deep for that. Man does not love God, and neither does he love his neighbor. But the gospel declared in Ephesians presents the answer: peace with God and peace from God.

Watchman Nee tells of a Chinese Christian who had his rice field on a hill. Every day he had to hand-work a water wheel to lift water from the irrigation stream at the base of the hill. His neighbor had two fields below his, and one night he made a hole in the wall that separated their property so that the Christian's water would all drain down into his fields. The Christian was understandably angry, but he wanted to honor God, and so he took the matter to his church. There, the Christians reasoned that if he retaliated, he would be little different from everybody else. Wanting to show that peace with God gave him peace in his struggles with his fellow man, the Christian decided what to do. The next day he went down to the water wheel and first pumped water into his neighbor's two fields and then, working late into the day, filled his own fields. When he was done his neighbor came out to ask why he would possibly do such a thing, and that conversation ultimately led to the man's conversion to Christianity.[15] The Christian had peace with God, and he extended that peace to his fellow, sinful man. We need to do the same, and especially to live in peace with our brothers and sisters in the family of God.

Men and women are at war not just with God, and not just with others, but also within themselves. Isaiah 57:20–21 says:

> "But the wicked are like the tossing sea;
>   for it cannot be quiet,
>   and its waters toss up mire and dirt.
> There is no peace," says my God, "for the wicked."

Humanity in sin is pulled apart, with an internal conflict we cannot subdue. Sin makes us slaves of the world and the devil, of the cravings of the flesh—that is how Paul describes us in Ephesians 2—and yet we are not able to escape our knowledge of God and our need for him or the reality that we were made in his image and for his pleasure. Isaiah put it exactly right—we are caught between two great influences like the churning sea with the earth and the moon each pulling it, with no peace of mind, no rest of spirit, no satisfaction of heart. Like the ocean when it meets the shore, our waves churn up mire and muck.

Do you know something about that? Of course you do. We are made by God in such a way that we can have peace within ourselves only when and as we have peace with him. You will never have peace in rebellion against God, by doing

11

things your own way, establishing your position as the captain of your own soul. No, peace comes only through submission to the Almighty, by faith in the Savior who removes the enmity and sends God's Spirit of peace. This is why Paul is able to tell Christians, even in the midst of the greatest turmoil this life can bring, in the face of death and poverty and sorrow and storm, that through faith in Christ they may approach God himself for help. This is why a Christian can face the terrible news of a fatal disease, the loss of a job, persecution from the world—peace from God! Paul writes in Philippians 4:7, "And the peace of God, which surpasses all understanding, will guard your hearts and your minds in Christ Jesus." What we so desperately need is the peace of God, which comes only through peace with God through Jesus Christ, the peacemaker.

GRACE TO YOU

How do we gain this peace? How are we to have peace with God and therefore the peace of God? The answer is God's grace. Can we repair our broken relationship with God? Can we perform works to appease God? No, for nothing we can ever do removes the guilt of our past sins, and nothing we do is free from the stain of sinful motives and corruption. In short, we cannot save ourselves—this is the true problem Paul sets before us in Ephesians—and God must therefore save us. Ephesians 2:4 explains this, first drawing out the true extent of our problem in sin but then pointing to our only hope: "God, being rich in mercy." Our hope of salvation, our pathway to peace, is the grace of God, who is rich in mercy.

This is the first sense in which we should consider this matter of grace, as something in God, an outworking of God's attributes of goodness and mercy. "God is love," said the apostle John (1 John 4:8). Paul says in Romans 5:8, "God shows his love for us in that while we were still sinners, Christ died for us." Grace is often defined as God's unmerited favor. That is true, but it does not go far enough. Grace is God's favor to us when we have merited the opposite. We have earned his hatred and wrath and condemnation. And yet he causes us to be forgiven and made his precious children. He brings us into his household and lavishes us with every good thing. He gives that which is most precious to himself—his only Son— that he might remove our offense on the cross and by his blood reconcile us to God. This is the measure of God's grace, and Paul wants us to learn this in our study of Ephesians. "I pray," he writes in Ephesians 3:17–18, "that you . . . may have power . . . to grasp how wide and long and high and deep is the love of Christ" (NIV). We are saved by God's grace alone, he says in Ephesians 2:8, not by our works but by God's gift; not because we loved him, for we have not loved God, but because he loved us and sent his Son to bear our sins and to be our peace.

Thus when Paul says, "Grace to you . . . from God our Father and the Lord Jesus Christ," he first means the grace in God that motivates him to save us. But he also means the whole redemptive plan of God, the grace by which he has worked in history to plan and accomplish and then apply his redemptive purpose for us. That is what we will soon consider in detail as we get into Ephesians 1. God planned our redemption before the creation of the world, choosing us in Christ for holiness and predestinating us to be his children (Eph. 1:4–5). When the right time had come, he sent his Son, Jesus Christ, to redeem us from our sins and gain our forgiveness (Eph. 1:7). Then he brought us to the realization of this salvation at a particular point in time through the gift of faith, making known to us this mystery of his will (Eph. 1:9). Now, he is working in us by the Holy Spirit for the completion of what is but a beginning (Eph. 1:13–14). Here is God's grace, a great and unstoppable plan for our salvation, a grace on which we may utterly rely and which is all, as Paul sums up in Ephesians 1:14, "to the praise of his glory."

Finally, grace is God's power working in us for newness of life. This, too, Paul greatly desires that we should learn in Ephesians. His prayer at the end of Ephesians 1 makes this clear. He prays that "having the eyes of your hearts enlightened, . . . you may know what is the hope to which he has called you, what are the riches of his glorious inheritance in the saints, and what is the immeasurable greatness of his power toward us who believe, according to the working of his great might that he worked in Christ when he raised him from the dead" (Eph. 1:18–20). God has grace for us, resurrection power to live as children of light, a redeemed people living holy lives to the praise of his name.

This is the good news worked out in this Book of Ephesians, Paul's gospel of Jesus Christ. We might summarize it all in this way: "Peace through grace in Jesus Christ." Have you received the grace of God for your salvation? Are you able to say you have peace with God, and as a result you increasingly know the peace of God? Do you increasingly possess love and harmony with other people, peace and calm and joy and contentment within your heart? Do you have power for new obedience, grace for fellowship with God? If you do, it is only because of God's grace, and you should praise him with the whole of your life. If you do not, you need only ask him for it, for God freely gives his grace to all who come through Jesus Christ, trusting him to be their peace, to the praise of God in his glorious grace.

2

WHAT IS A CHRISTIAN?

Ephesians 1:1

Paul, an apostle of Christ Jesus by the will of God, To the saints who are in Ephesus, and are faithful in Christ Jesus.
—Ephesians 1:1

In 1738, John Wesley boarded a ship in the British colony of Georgia to return home to England after two years as a Christian missionary. During the long voyage home, he had plenty of time to reflect on his life. He looked back over his time at Oxford, where he was ordained a priest in the Church of England and where he distinguished himself for his leadership of the Holy Club. These zealous young men met nightly to study the Bible and devoted themselves to good works. This was followed by arduous missionary work in the New World. With these credentials it is a surprise to read what Wesley wrote in his journal:

> It is now two years and almost four months since I left my native country in order to teach the Georgian Indians the nature of Christianity; but what have I learned myself in the meantime? Why, what I least suspected, that I, who went to America to covert others, was myself never converted to God!

Wesley had come to realize that for all his religious attainments—his degrees, his associations, his morality, his works—he lacked a saving relationship with Jesus Christ. Though an eminent member of the church, he was not a Christian. Wesley began searching for true salvation, and it was not long before he found it in the gospel of God's grace and especially in the precious blood of Christ. Wesley records what it was like when he finally found true and saving faith:

> I felt my heart strangely warmed. I felt I did trust in Christ, Christ alone for salvation; and an assurance was given me that He had taken away *my* sins, even *mine,* and saved *me* from the law of sin and death.[1]

Wesley's experience is an important one for us to reflect upon, because many people in the church today are in the situation he was in. They have read the Bible, they have given time and labor and money to the cause of religion, but they have never ceased relying on themselves, their works, their goodness, and as a result they have never truly been saved.

This matter would undoubtedly have interested the apostle Paul. I say this because of the great labor he exerts in Ephesians to describe what a Christian really is. Paul puts it several ways: Christians are the body of Christ, the family of God, a holy nation, and a temple in which God lives. Christians are those who are chosen in God's love, adopted as his children, and forgiven by Christ's blood. The Christian is the "new man," part of the new society in the new creation of Christ's resurrection life. Paul wants us to know what it means to be a Christian, what are the glories and the resources and the obligations involved in a saving relationship with Jesus Christ. The first consideration must be, therefore, the description and definition of a Christian—and Paul provides a convenient answer to that question here in this opening verse. "To the saints who are in Ephesus, and are the faithful in Christ Jesus," he writes. These words will be the focus of our attention as we seek to answer the question, What is a Christian?

TO THE SAINTS

Few Bible words have a sadder history than the first word Paul uses to describe a Christian: "to the saints." Most people think of saints as superspiritual people who are far removed from the mundane affairs of life. How common it is to hear Christians exclaim, "I'm not a saint, after all!" But as Paul and the Bible use the word, you cannot be a Christian unless you are a saint. Being a Christian makes you a saint by definition.

We need to consider the Roman Catholic teaching here, because it exerts such a strong influence on most people's use of this word. Saints, they say, are those few whose spiritual excellence and merit cause them to be set before the church "as models and intercessors."[2] That last designation is important, because according to Rome these saints pray in heaven for those who call on them. "We can and should ask them to intercede for us," says the current Roman Catholic catechism.[3] People select patron saints and give names of saints to their children; in this manner, says Rome, "we are assured of [the saint's] intercession."[4] "They do not cease to intercede with

17

the Father for us," we are told, "as they proffer the merits which they acquired on earth."[5]

As a result, saints are venerated, a practice that Rome denies amounts to their worship in the place of God. But in practice, one commonly finds Roman Catholics praying to the saints instead of to God, seeking help and salvation from and offering praise to mere dead human beings. The idolatry of this practice lies on the very surface. Furthermore, the idea that anyone may come to God on his or her own merits, much less with excess merits—as Rome asserts regarding the saints—is offensive to the biblical idea of sin and of justification through faith alone and denies the sufficiency of Christ as our Savior and intercessor. It flies in the face of Paul's plain statement in 1 Timothy 2:5, "For there is one God, and there is one mediator between God and men, the man Christ Jesus." Harry Ironside, the great evangelist, in a letter to a Roman Catholic priest, rightly wrote of Christ as the only intercessor we need:

> Those who have confided in him as their savior need no other mediator than himself, for he is ever available, his heart is as tender as when here on earth, his love ever flows out to all his own. We need no other intermediary, neither his mother after the flesh, nor any saint or angel to entreat him on our behalf. He himself abides forever. . . . He is our great all-compassionate high priest with God, our advocate with the Father, our one mediator, excluding every other.[6]

Therefore we must not think of saints as superior Christians who offer their merits for us to God, but in Paul's use all Christians are saints. He uses this expression many times in his letters, and a glance through them will show that he means ordinary, regular, sinful, struggling Christians like you and me. First Corinthians presents a classic example, for Paul upbraids

18

those Christians for the grossest immorality. Yet he addresses even this letter to "saints" (1 Cor. 1:2).

The word *saint* comes from the Latin word *sanctus* and means "holy one." Holy means set apart by and for God. In this sense we must realize that sainthood is a fact concerning every Christian, something that has happened to all who are in Christ. Leon Morris explains, "The essential idea . . . is that of being set apart for God. A holy place, such as a temple, is a building not to be used for secular purposes; it is set apart for the worship of God. Holy vessels are withdrawn from all other use and are used only in the service of God. Similarly, 'saints' are people who belong to God."[7]

It is God who makes us saints, who separates us and calls us from the world. Likewise all Christians are set apart for God, by God. *Saints* describes something that has happened to us. We have been set apart for God, we are made his, we are his property and his holy people. Peter writes in 1 Peter 2:10, "Once you were not a people, but now you are God's people." We are saints. We are holy unto God. That is what we are.

Sainthood is a fact concerning Christians, but it is also a calling and an obligation. Those who are separated to God are thereby called to live holy lives. By definition a Christian is different from someone who is not a Christian. He or she is separated not from people but from sin, not from the world itself but from the principle of worldliness. If you do not want to be different, you cannot be a Christian. D. Martyn Lloyd-Jones writes:

> You cannot be a saint and a Christian without being separated in some radical sense from the world. You do not belong to it any longer, you are in it but you are not of it. . . . There is a separation which has taken place in your mind, in your outlook, in your heart, in your conversation, in your behavior. You are essentially

a different person; the Christian is not a worldly person, he is not governed by the world and its mind and outlook.[8]

This is to be increasingly true in the character of our lives. Do you find this to be true of you: that you no longer think in the way you used to, that you don't respond to things the way you used to, that you have new and godly pleasures and interests and pursuits that mark you out as different in the world? Are you becoming more holy? If you are, this shows that God has separated you to himself, that he has made you a saint.

TO THE FAITHFUL

Paul's second description of the Christian is *the faithful*. He does not mean those who are trustworthy, who can be relied upon, but those who live and come to God by means of faith. The New Testament constantly stresses faith—the need to believe the message, to believe the gospel, to look to God in faith in order to be saved.

This tells us that to be a Christian you must believe certain things. So much of the New Testament is devoted to presenting truths we must accept and rely upon, to refuting error, to opposing false teaching and asserting truth so that people may believe and become Christians. You are not a Christian if you are simply a charitable person, if you lead a certain lifestyle, because of a moral quality or idealism. You are a Christian if you believe certain specific and essential truths, truths that center on the Lord Jesus Christ.

Paul stresses this constantly in his letters. A clear example comes at the beginning of 1 Corinthians 15, in which he says, "Now, I would remind you, brothers, of the gospel I preached to you, which you received, in which you stand, and by which you are being saved, if you hold fast to the word I preached to you—unless you believed in vain" (1 Cor. 15:1–2). There are certain truths you must believe; believing otherwise will leave you unsaved. He goes on to give a short list: "that Christ died for our sins . . . that he was buried, that he was raised on the third day . . . that he appeared to Cephas, then to the twelve" (1 Cor. 15:3–5). People say, "I am a Christian, but I just don't believe in the resurrection"; Paul says, You are not a Christian unless you do. Furthermore, we must believe not just facts but also the doctrine tied to these facts. Jesus did not simply die; he died "for our sins," not merely as a moral example or as a statement of God's love for us but as a substitute, a sacrifice of atonement. The doctrine of substitutionary atonement is essential to Christianity; without believing it you are not a Christian.

What, then, does it mean to believe? Classically, there are three elements to saving faith, beginning with knowledge. It is not enough to simply mouth words, to follow some liturgy or go through some religious motions. A man was asked what he believed. He replied, "I believe what the church believes." He then was asked, "Well, what does the church believe?" "The church believes what I believe." "Okay, then what do you and the church believe?" The man finally said, "We believe the same thing!" That is not faith, for faith requires knowledge and understanding. This is why we must emphasize teaching in the church, to explain what sin means and what it means that Jesus died for our sins on the cross and other vital truths.

Next comes belief or assent. There are people who have knowledge, who understand and can explain Christian truth perfectly well, but they don't believe it. Many scholars are like this. They know it and can teach it. They understand the theory of the virgin birth and incarnation, the atonement of Christ, the resurrection and new birth, yet they don't accept these doctrines. But faith requires belief.

Third, and this is essential, saving faith requires personal commitment. It is not enough to believe in sin; we must acknowledge that *we* are sinners. It is not enough to assent that Christ is a Savior; he must be *our* Savior. This is why John Wesley's conversion was so credible; he spoke of *my* sin, *my* salvation, *my* Savior, and so must we.

We must not merely assent to truth. We must embrace Jesus, trusting him, relying on God's promises, committing our hope and salvation into his pierced hands and onto his shed blood. The story is told of a dry, academic preacher who suddenly broke out in tears in the middle of his sermon; one of the people exclaimed, "The preacher converted himself!" And it was true! Saving faith involves personal commitment; it involves the heart as well as the head. Believing God's Word we give ourselves to Christ and take him as our own. We commit ourselves and our souls to his eternal safekeeping.

Are you looking for something to believe in, for someone to trust? This, you know, is the great want of our time. A recent survey of teenagers asked, "What do you wish for most in your life?" Do you know what the answer was? It wasn't money, it wasn't success, it wasn't pleasure. "What do you most want?" they were asked. The number one answer was, "Someone we can trust."[9] The cultural tragedy of our time is no one to trust, but you may turn to Jesus Christ and trust him with your heart, with your mind, with your life, with your eternal soul. If you are looking for someone to trust, you are looking for him. Have you believed and trusted him? He said, "I am the way, and the truth, and the life" (John 14:6); he is the Savior who will never let you down, never let you go, never fail your need. Trust him, and you will be saved.

Faith does not save us; Jesus Christ saves us. For this reason, we should think of faith as being primarily receptive. It receives Christ and his saving work for us. The hymn "Rock of Ages" aptly describes how faith makes us Christians: "Nothing in my hand I bring, simply to thy cross I cling."[10] Faith trusts and receives, open-handedly grasping what is promised and offered by God in Jesus Christ. We are not saved by our faith, but we are saved through our faith as it brings us to the Savior, Jesus Christ. He saves us. Faith brings us to him and lays hold of him for salvation.

But once brought to Jesus, our faith becomes an active principle and force. Believing these truths, we begin to act upon them; committing ourselves to Christ, we manifest that commitment in our choices and actions and lives. We are thus called to be faithful to him, reliable in his service, ready to defend the truth, to obey what he commands. As with holiness, so also with faith: that which is first objective and heavenward must then be manifest in the realm of the subjective and the earthly. "To the saints," the "faithful," Paul writes, meaning every Christian, as a description of what we are, but also as a high calling for our lives.

IN CHRIST JESUS

One of the great Pauline expressions, one that is important to his thought, is "in Christ." This is our third description: Christians are saints, they are people of faith, but most importantly they are people in Christ Jesus.

Faith is in Christ as he is the object of our faith; we believe in him. But Paul mainly has in mind a union of representative or covenant headship. This means that what Christ did, he did for us, on our behalf, applying to us the benefits of his redemptive work. Faith is in Christ, and faith places us into Christ as our covenant head.

The Old Testament shows this as a great pattern of God's redemptive work. Genesis 15 records God making a covenant with Abraham for his salvation and the salvation of others through him. If you wanted to be saved in that time, if you wanted to enter God's redemptive work, you had to be in Abraham. You had to come and enter his tents, place yourselves under Abraham's authority, receive the covenant mark of circumcision if you were a male, serve and trust the God of Abraham. If you did that, if you entered into the faith of Abraham, you were saved according to God's covenant with him. This passed on to his descendants, so that salvation was in Abraham, in Isaac, and then in Jacob.

Jacob's sons became the twelve tribes of Israel. If you wanted to be right with God and receive his blessings, you had to join Israel in the exodus and go with Israel into the Promised Land. This was a legal relationship, a covenantal relationship, even a geographical relationship.

One of the great scenes that shows this comes from the Book of Ruth. Naomi and her husband and sons had left Israel to live in Moab, and her sons had taken Moabite wives, one of whom was Ruth. In the course of time all the men died, which probably insinuates what happened when you departed from the land of salvation, when you were no longer in Israel, leaving Naomi and her daughters-in-law. In the account where these women decided what to do and where to go, it is clear that the matter was not just one of shelter and food but of faith and salvation. To cross back over the Jordan meant to be in Israel and enter into covenant with Israel's Lord. Ruth's plea of union with Naomi is a beautiful statement of what it means for us to be in Christ: "Where you go I will go, and where you lodge I will lodge. Your people shall be my people, and your God my God. Where you die I will die, and there will I be buried" (Ruth 1:16–17). Ruth went with Naomi into Israel and received such salvation that Naomi's and Israel's God would provide.

Later, God entered into covenant with David and with the tribe of Judah, and salvation thenceforth was of the Jews. When the kingdom was divided and the ten tribes rebelled against David's grandson, the faithful of all the other tribes

24

left their homes to come to Judah, for salvation was in David and in that tribe (2 Chron. 11:13–17).

You see, then, something of what it means to be in Christ. A Christian is one who comes to Jesus seeking salvation through him, serving him and receiving from him the benefits of his redemption. We come to serve him, to enter into his discipleship, like Ruth with Naomi, going with him, staying with him, dying with him, but also sharing in the resurrection life he has to give.

To receive Christ as Savior, we must come to him to be our Lord. We come into his castle, as it were; we place our sword at his feet, our hand on our heart, and proffer our oath of fealty. We fly his banner from our masts. We become his disciples and call him Master. In turn he becomes our Savior, that we might partake of the great redemptive blessings he offers to us, that we might eat of his table and have fellowship with him. Salvation is in Christ. It is having come to Jesus as our Lord and thus seeking the salvation he has to give. "This is the new covenant in my blood," he said, passing the cup to his disciples. It is as we sit at his table that he our Lord dispenses to us the salvation he has gained in covenant with God the Father.

This is an objective reality. You are either in Christ or you are not. Here, again, a medieval way of thinking is helpful. Whose livery do you wear? Whose coat of arms emblazons your heart? In whose righteousness do you stand before God? It is an objective thing, and God sees it all quite plainly. You are either in Christ or you are not. Paul writes, "The Lord knows those who are his" (2 Tim. 2:19), and they are in Christ. So the questions are, Are you in Christ? Whose flag waves above your heart? Whose loyalty have you sworn? Whose cause do you trust and serve? Whose name do you love?

This is what ultimately matters in life. Your salvation does not depend on your subjective experience or feelings. You may be happy or sad, you may be strong or weak, you may be filled with confidence or wracked with doubt. These things matter to you, and they certainly are significant. But they do not determine your salvation. The question is Are you in Christ? Are you happy in Christ, taking your joys to him with thanks? Are you sad in Christ, bathing his feet with your tears? The question is not your feelings, which change from day to day, but Who is your Lord? To whom have you come for salvation?

In Ephesus, in Christ

The apostle speaks to readers who are in two places. They are in Ephesus, and they are in Christ. I said in the last chapter that the words *in Ephesus* probably do not belong in the text and that this letter likely had a broader audience than just the Ephesians. But nonetheless, those first readers were in two realms: they were in Ephesus or one of the nearby towns, and they were in Christ as well.

The same is true of you. In one sense there is nothing special about you. You look and dress and act like everybody else. You are in a certain place, a certain city or town, along with many others. You derive benefits and accept obligations from this, and all of this is obvious to everyone. But what is perceived only by faith, what is realized only by faith, is what God has done to make you holy unto him, what God has done to take you out of this world—not physically but covenantally and spiritually—and brought you into Christ. You are no longer bound up with the fate of this passing, dying, cursed world that is under God's wrath. You are in Christ, by God's grace and through faith, so that what is his is now yours. You no longer partake of the spirit of this world and age, following its ways and its cravings and rules, but you are spiritually joined to Christ, with his life moving in yours for a new life.

To put this differently, we may be in the world, in Ephesus or elsewhere, but a Christian is one who is no longer of it. Our supreme interest, our home, our hope is with Christ and in Christ. The love of Christ and his heaven is even now driving out the love of the world and the things of the world. Though we live here now, we do so representing Christ, serving Christ, trusting Christ, and waiting for Christ with one eye on the horizon for the day when this present world will be no more, when the only world will be the one in Christ, to the praise of God the Father. That is what a Christian is.

Surely Paul desires us to reflect on these things and on our lives, to do what John Wesley did on that boat. Am I a Christian? he asked. Am I in Christ? God forbid that any of us should fail to gain a clear and definite answer to that question, that we should fail to come to Jesus, as the sinners that we are, claiming him as Lord and receiving from him through faith the salvation of our souls.

3

BLESSING FOR
BLESSING

Ephesians 1:3

*Blessed be the God and Father of our
Lord Jesus Christ, who has blessed us in Christ with
every spiritual blessing in the heavenly places.*
—Ephesians 1:3

The apostle Paul's letters are marked by a depth and coherence of thought and by an impetuous and exuberant fervor. Some people today want to separate the head from the heart, but for Paul such a disconnect was unthinkable. It was the thoughts in his head that set his heart on fire. One writer says, "Put a pen into his hand and it is like tapping a blast furnace; and out rushes a fiery stream at white heat."[1] If this is true of Paul's letters generally, it is especially true of

29

this epistle to the Ephesians. This first chapter, especially, is as robust in its doctrinal teaching as it is inspiring in the heights that it achieves. At the beginning of this letter, Paul's greeting gives way to a hymn of praise to God for the blessings of salvation that is one of the most instructive and inspiring passages in all of Scripture.

Ephesians 1:3 begins a long section of praise that continues through to Ephesians 1:14. We should make some preliminary observations, beginning with the fact that in the original Greek text these twelve verses form a single long sentence. From the beginning of verse 3 to the end of verse 14 is one cascading overflow of prose and praise. Some scholars criticize this for the supposedly poor Greek style; one writes that this passage is "the most monstrous sentence conglomeration that I have ever found in the Greek language."[2] We are reminded of similar criticisms leveled against Paul in his day; rather than depending on the structure and style of formal rhetoric, the apostle relied on bare, impassioned truth. In 2 Corinthians 4:2 he explains, "By the open statement of the truth we would commend ourselves to everyone's conscience in the sight of God." In this respect few of Paul's passages rival the one before us. F. R. Barry calls it "a swirl of words with a storm of thought behind them."[3]

This section of Ephesians reveals the trinitarian structure of Paul's thinking. Ephesians 1:3–6 focus on God the Father ordaining salvation; Ephesians 1:7–12 speak of God the Son's work in redeeming us from sin; and Ephesians 1:13–14 tell of God the Spirit applying that salvation to individuals. But even while we acknowledge Paul's trinitarianism, we are wrong to understand him viewing the various divine persons working in isolation. Quite to the contrary, all through this passage Paul presents them acting in concert.

For this reason, B. B. Warfield persuasively argues that

this hymn is structured on a temporal basis, with salvation considered from eternity past to eternity future. First is God's sovereign election in the past councils of eternity; next is God's redemptive achievement in the first coming of Christ; next is the sealing of these benefits to individuals in the present age; finally, is the future eternal gathering of all things in him, "things in heaven and things on earth" (Eph. 1:10). At different stages one of the members of the Trinity may be in the foreground, but the work of each remains constantly in view: God the Father ordaining, God the Son achieving, God the Spirit applying.

However we view Paul's structure in this passage, his goals are transparent. Two objectives leap off the page, the first of which is that we as believers might know our blessings. Ephesians 1:3 speaks of "every spiritual blessing," and Paul goes to great length to spell these out. Few things are more important for believers to know and understand than the rich blessings that are ours in Jesus Christ: blessings in the past, blessings in the present, blessings in the future, all securely provided by God. We will spend several chapters working through this passage, coming to know, as Paul later prays, what is "the hope to which he has called you" (Eph. 1:18).

Paul's second objective has to do with our response to such knowledge, one of adoring praise that is lifted up to God. Ephesians 1:3 begins Paul's hymn with a progression of ideas build around the word *bless*. *"Blessed* be God," Paul begins, drawing our attention to God's worthiness to be praised. He then tells us why: "who has *blessed* us." In what way? "In Christ with every spiritual *blessing.*" Warfield observes, "When a man's lips can frame only this one word—'Blessing, blessing, blessing!' we know what is in his heart."[4] Paul would have the same be said of us as we enter into our study of the fullness of God's saving blessing in Christ in this magnificent exclamation of praise in Ephesians 1.

THE SOURCE OF OUR BLESSING

Focusing on Ephesians 1:3, we first should consider the source or origin of our blessing. From where do these salvation blessings come? The plain answer is that they have their origin in God. The nineteenth-century Scotsman Hugh Martin explains, "The context very emphatically answers the question and very steadily keeps the answer under our attention. They originate in the mere grace and good pleasure of God, his unfettered, undeserved sovereign love."[5] We see this in Ephesians 1:3, where we bless, or praise, God because he "has blessed us." Paul spells this out with great specificity in the verses that follow, saying that our salvation is "according to the purpose of his will" (Eph. 1:5). It is "to the praise of his glorious grace" that he has blessed us (Eph. 1:6); God has "lavished" salvation on us (Eph. 1:8); it is "according to his purpose" (Eph. 1:9), "according to the purpose of him who works out all things according to the counsel of his will" (Eph. 1:11). Paul could not have expressed more extravagantly the great truth stated simply in James 1:17: "Every good gift and every perfect gift is from above, coming down from the Father of lights."

Note, too, the emphasis not merely on God as the source of salvation's blessings but specifically on God the Father. "Blessed be the God and Father of our Lord Jesus Christ," Paul says (Eph. 1:3). This warns us from a grave error so common in many people's experience, namely, to attribute our salvation to God the Son—to Jesus Christ—while considering God the Father a reluctant and somewhat skeptical participant. We think of Jesus pleading his merits for us in heaven, and we wrongly conclude the thrice-holy Father must be ill-disposed toward us, watching for a slip-up, aching for an opportunity to chastise, distant in his affections for unworthies such as us.

But how wrong this is, and what a significant error! If God

the Son took our sins upon the cross it was because this was the specific task the Father sent him into the world to accomplish. Speaking of this assigned work, Jesus prayed just before his arrest, "I glorified you on earth, having accomplished the work that you gave me to do" (John 17:4). John 3:16 says, "For God so loved the world, that he gave his only Son, that whoever believes in him should not perish but have eternal life." We are made God's children through Christ because "in love [the Father] predestined us for adoption" (Eph. 1:5). Ephesians 1:7 tells us "we have redemption through [Christ's] blood . . . according to the riches of [the Father's] grace."

What a difference this makes in terms of our security in salvation. There is no debate raging within the Godhead concerning our place in salvation, no tension; there are no awkward silences or heated conversations. Rather there is a grand and cohesive conspiracy of love originating in the eternal and sovereign grace of the Father. The apostle John says, "We know and rely on the love God has for us" (1 John 4:16 NIV). How greatly we need to know God's love in a world such as ours, in the weakness and failure of our lives. How certain it is that we will know the joy meant for us only by relying on his tender fatherly affection, which Paul sets before us as such an object of faith and of praise.

All our blessings have their source in the grace of God the Father, his sovereign and free gift of love to us. For this reason all the praise belongs to him; all of salvation is "to the praise of his glorious grace" (Eph. 1:6). God's grace is the origin of our blessings, and the end purpose of our being blessed is that he should be praised because of this grace. Martin writes that our salvation blessings "are designed to promote the manifestation of the glory of God and especially of his grace. This is the end that God has in view in blessing us with all spiritual blessings. . . . He designs thereby to make his own glory manifest, to make it resplendent and conspicuous. He proposes to give an eternal exhibition of the greatness and glory of his grace." Martin concludes from this:

> Can anything be more encouraging? . . . Can it possibly consist with the honour, the infinite dignity, the glory of God that I should be forgiven, accepted, adopted, renewed, sanctified and made an heir of glory? . . . And does not this constrain my wonder, joy, surprise and praise, that I should be called not only to receive freely an infinite, sovereign, undeserved love, but that my reception of it should be the means of throwing light, to the angelic beings, during the eternal ages, on the glorious character and perfections of God?[6]

THE NATURE OF OUR BLESSING

Salvation's blessings all come from God the Father. Next we should consider the nature of these blessings. What kind of blessing does the apostle have in mind? Ephesians 1:3 tells us: "every spiritual blessing." Christians derive many material or temporal blessings from God. Jesus tells us in the Sermon on the Mount not to be anxious for anything because God carefully considers our every need. Paul writes in Philippians 4:19, "My God will supply every need of yours according to his riches in glory in Christ Jesus."

But what causes Paul to ring forth with specific praise to God is the spiritual blessing that belongs to every Christian. There is some debate as to what Paul means by "spiritual." The commentators are divided, some seeing an emphasis on the Holy Spirit as the medium of blessings, so that they are "the Spirit's blessings." Others see an emphasis on those blessings that are spiritual in character. There is no need for us to choose between the two. It is obvious from what follows that Paul especially thinks of blessings that are spiritual rather than material, all of which come through the Holy Spirit's sealing and applying work.

Paul praises God for every spiritual blessing, all of which every believer may fully partake. There is no difference among believers when it comes to these spiritual blessings; all of them are for all of us. That is not God's design with material blessings. God makes some people rich and others poor; some live in comfort and others in anguish. But every believer may bless God for the whole of the spiritual blessings with which he has blessed us in Jesus Christ.

What a difference it makes, for instance, to know that my sins are forgiven. Psalm 32 rightly begins, "Blessed is the one whose transgression is forgiven, whose sin is covered." Here is a peace of mind that no amount of money can buy, that no pleasure or fame can replace. And there is no Christian who cannot revel in this spiritual blessing. The same is true of the blessing of divine election. However much the world may revile us, Christians are told of God's free and sovereign love, forged in the eternal furnace of his changeless will. What a blessing is that! You may be poor, you may be robbed or mistreated, you may be hated and reviled, but the Scripture stands true: "In the house of the righteous there is much treasure" (Prov. 15:6). There with the child of God is the presence of God's Spirit and the Father's blessing and the saving blood of Christ.

Do you know these blessings? Do they sustain you in the trials of this life? Do they keep your heart from an inordinate love of this world? As God is a Spirit, his chief blessings are spiritual in keeping with his nature. In heaven our rewards will be spiritual—the sight of God's face, a crown of glory that never fades away. Paul therefore writes, "Though outwardly we are wasting away, yet inwardly we are being renewed day by day. For our light and momentary troubles are achieving for us an eternal glory that far outweighs them all" (2 Cor. 4:16–17 NIV).

All of these spiritual blessings we apprehend now by faith,

and Paul stresses here not merely our future enjoyment of spiritual blessings but also their present possession. "God . . . has blessed us." What one day will be fully manifest in heaven was long ago ordained by God and then secured by his Son Jesus Christ, so that by faith and in the power of the Spirit, we might receive and enjoy even now these glorious blessings.

THE LOCATION OF OUR BLESSING

Third, Paul makes a definite statement regarding the location of our blessing. He says God has blessed us "in the heavenly places." This is an expression we are going to encounter again in Ephesians, and Paul never spells out exactly what he means. It is clear, however, that he is not only talking about our future life in heaven, for in Ephesians 6:12 he will speak of our spiritual combat with evil powers taking place now "in the heavenly places." John Stott therefore defines "the heavenly places" as "the unseen world of spiritual reality."[7]

We earlier saw that the recipients of this letter were in two places: they were in Ephesus, and they were in Christ Jesus. This is key to understanding Paul's point here. Jesus told Pilate, "My kingdom is not of this world" (John 18:36). His kingdom is spiritual and unseen. It is future in consummation but presently real to those who have faith in him. Paul stresses in Philippians 3:20 that while we live here, "our citizenship is in heaven." Our hope, our interest, our future are in the heavenly realms, and even now that is where our spiritual blessings are found and enjoyed.

Like the original readers, we are in two realms, that of this present world and that of Christ's kingdom. It is in the latter that these spiritual blessings are manifest. Let's take one for instance. Spiritually, in the heavenly realms, we are blessed with adoption as children of God. That is true of us now, but it is not manifest in this earthly sphere. No royal robes fall from our shoulders. No visible insignia marks us out as royal sons and daughters. Angels minister to our needs, yet no eye beholds them. No crowds gather to watch as we pass by, we who are chosen for eternal inheritance with Christ; no spellbound readers follow the day-to-day progress of our pilgrimage to glory; no hands reach out to touch our persons cleansed white and made resplendent by the shed blood of God's Son. How odd all this is from the perspective of the heavenly realm; into these things angels inquire with wonder! Eternity will record the world's disinterest and scorn of us as an oddity and a cause for its condemnation.

Likewise, the victory that is ours in Christ makes little visible impression on our earthly lives. Wearily we battle temptation. Painfully we toil under diseases and afflictions that take no notice of our citizenship in heaven. Ultimately, death will place its bony hands upon us as if we were common rabble; our spiritual blessings will not keep us from the grave. Yet all the while are these great riches in the heavenly places. They are spiritual, and they are real, and they strengthen us for all the trials of this worldly life.

Here is this incongruity, this seeming contradiction so evident in our experiences, that seeks to deny the spiritual realities in heavenly realms. To so many, our worldly experience pleads the necessity of unbelief. How can we believe there are blessings in the heavenly places when our life is filled with pain and sorrow? But we instead plead the blessings that are ours through faith alone. "In this world you will have trouble," Jesus forewarned. "But," he added, "take heart! I have overcome the world" (John 16:33 NIV). Therefore by faith we raise our spirits. We take our minds and hearts up to where our bodies now cannot go, into the heavenlies, where spiritual blessings wait for us.

Therefore, these two statements go together inseparably: in the heavenly places and in Christ. What is the location of these blessings? They are in the heavenlies, but also they are in Jesus Christ. Paul writes in Ephesians 1:20–22 that when God raised Jesus from the dead, he seated him "at his right hand in the heavenly places, far above all rule and authority and power and dominion, and above every name that is named, not only in this age but also in the one to come. And he put all things under his feet and gave him as head over all things to the church." Jesus Christ is now Lord of the unseen realm; all the blessings that reside in the heavenlies are under his authority and control for the sake of his people.

What this means is that we must go to Christ for these spiritual blessings. Where is Christ? He is at God's right hand in the heavenly realms. We go to him in the only possible way, by faith through the ministry of the Holy Spirit. To seek blessings in the heavenlies is to seek blessings in Christ, from Christ, in communion with Christ, in reliance on his saving work for us.

It is noteworthy that Paul refers to God as "the God and Father of our Lord Jesus Christ." This tells us that it is only through Jesus Christ that the God becomes our God, that the heavenly Father becomes our Father and we his children. Jesus stated this pointedly to Mary Magdalene, before his ascension: "I am ascending to my Father and your Father, to my God and your God" (John 20:17). There is no saving relationship with God the Father except through God the Son, Jesus Christ, the Savior who died for sinners, the Lord who was raised from the grave to rule the heavenly realms for the sake of his church, the one Mediator who reconciles sinners from condemnation to membership in the family of God.

The importance to the apostle of Jesus Christ as the only One in whom all God's blessings are found is demonstrated by the frequency with which Paul mentions him. We are only in verse 3 of Ephesians 1, and Paul already has mentioned Christ four times. In this protracted, twelve-verse sentence, he makes explicit mention of Jesus, one way or another, fifteen times. All the blessings are from God the Father and in Christ.

We might use a business analogy if we do not press it too far, namely, that God the Father is the producer of all the spiritual goods, out of his eternal counsel all our blessings are made, and Jesus Christ is the sole distributor, licensed by the Father to alone dispense these blessings. "I am the way, and the truth, and the life," he said (John 14:6), and God's blessings are found in him alone.

Salvation's blessings are all in Christ because they were given first to him that we might find our blessing in union with him by faith. "Christ himself is God's great and unspeakable gift," wrote Martin.

> How rich and glorious, then, is Christ, considered as the treasure-house of all spiritual blessings. In him we find laid up for us election, adoption, acceptance, redemption, inheritance, the Spirit's unction, seal and earnest. He is the Elect, the Son, the Beloved, the Redeemer, the Heir, the Anointed and Sealed of the Spirit. . . . We are elect in Christ the Elect One, sons in Christ the Son, accepted in the Beloved, redeemed in the Redeemer, heirs in the Elder Brother, anointed and sealed in Christ.[8]

Jesus said, "I am the vine; you are the branches. Whoever abides in me and I in him, he it is that bears much fruit, for apart from me you can do nothing. . . . If you abide in me, and my words abide in you, ask whatever you wish, and it will be done for you. By this my Father is glorified, that you bear much fruit and so prove to be my disciples" (John 15:5–8). All salvation blessings are in Christ.

Obtaining God's Blessings

That leads us to an all-important question. How do you get these blessings for yourself? The answer is obvious from all we have said. If you want to be blessed in the heavenly realms with all the spiritual blessings in Christ, you must spiritually go to Christ, confess to him your need of his redeeming work, receive from him the spiritual blessing of forgiveness from sin, adoption as God's child, a certificate of eternal election, power for holiness of life, and a portion in the inheritance of God. John 3:36 tells us, "Whoever believes in the Son has eternal life; whoever does not obey the Son shall not see life, but the wrath of God remains on him."

Have you come to Christ for your salvation? If you have, then God would have you strengthen your life in this world through the blessings already yours in the heavenly realms. Do not live spiritually like a pauper through unbelief, when by faith you are in fact a child—a prince or princess—of the heavenly king.

If you have not come to Jesus, if you have not acknowledged him as Savior, if you have not confessed your personal need for him to take you to himself and give to you the blessings he alone can give, then you need to understand what this verse plainly implies. It is true that you may find blessings from God apart from Jesus Christ, but they are worldly ones only. God is good toward the world in common grace; he makes rain to fall and the sun to shine on the unjust as well as on the just. You may find in God's kind providence all the blessings this world has to give: wealth, fame, power, pleasure—blessings that will perish with this passing world. But of these spiritual blessings you will know nothing unless you are in Christ through faith in him. "For the kingdom of God is not a matter of eating and drinking," Paul wrote elsewhere, "but of righteousness and peace and joy in the Holy Spirit" (Rom. 14:17). This and much more will be yours if you will come to Jesus Christ, receiving God's saving blessings from him who came and died and rose again that we might have eternal life in him.

4

CHOSEN IN CHRIST

Ephesians 1:4

Even as he chose us in him before the foundation of the world,
that we should be holy and blameless before him.
—Ephesians 1:4

While I was ministering in the city of Philadelphia, some large construction projects took place there. As I occasionally passed by these sites I noticed how much work goes on before anything can be seen at ground level. Particularly with very tall buildings, a great deal of labor and care must be given to the foundation. If you want a building to stand fast, particularly one that reaches high into the sky, then you must dig deep and plant a firm foundation.

The apostle Paul shows a similar concern as he begins explaining the edifice of Christian salvation. Paul intends for us to see a work of the ages that is infinitely high, that reaches up into the precincts of infinity, that is shrouded in heavenly glory the way the highest peaks are clothed with mist and light. That is where Paul is headed as he begins this hymn of praise for the blessings of God. So he begins by digging deep, by setting the firmest possible foundation for what will reach up into heaven. God is leading us, Paul teaches, into eternity future, and so it is into eternity past that God sets the groundwork of our security. This is where the apostle begins as he counts the spiritual blessings that are ours in the heavenly places. He writes in Ephesians 1:4, "[God] chose us in him before the foundation of the world, that we should be holy and blameless before him."

THE DOCTRINE OF ELECTION

Ephesians 1:4 provides one of the clearest statements of what is known as the doctrine of election. This doctrine gets its name from the Greek word *eklektos,* the verb form of which is translated here as "he chose." What this verse and doctrine teach is that all the blessings we enjoy as Christians are grounded in the sovereign choosing of God, his sovereign election, which took place in eternity past, long before we were born and even before creation. Here is the foundation on which the salvation of every believer rests: God's free and gracious choice of us. This is the strongest, firmest foundation possible—God's eternal purpose—and it is upon this that Paul would have us ground our hope for salvation. John Calvin, who is known for teaching this doctrine, writes:

> God having chosen us before the world had its course, we must attribute the cause of our salvation to His free goodness; we must confess that He did not take us to be His children, for any deserts of our own; for we had nothing to recommend ourselves into His favor. There-

fore, we must put the cause and fountain of our salvation in Him only, and ground ourselves upon it.[1]

Paul tells us that our election took place "before the foundation of the world," and "in him," that is, "in Christ." I think the best way to understand this is to reflect upon the eternal covenant spoken of in the Bible. Along with God the Father and God the Spirit, God the Son existed in eternity past, long before he took on our flesh in the manger of Bethlehem. The Bible gives ample testimony that there was a covenant, or agreement, in eternity between God the Father and God the Son, established in a pre-creation council. Hebrews 13:20 refers to this as "the eternal covenant." Jesus mentioned it in his prayer on the night of his arrest: "[Father,] I glorified you on earth, having accomplished the work that you gave me to do" (John 17:4). Peter, likewise, speaks of Christ as the "lamb without blemish or spot . . . foreknown before the foundation of the world" (1 Peter 1:19–20). Revelation 13:8 calls Christ "the Lamb that was slain from the creation of the world" (NIV). These descriptions show us that even in eternity God dealt with the problem of sin and sinners. His grace for salvation extends back into the infinite depths before time. Election is in Christ's blood, for God foresaw and ordained not only that we would exist but also that we would need redemption from our sin. In choosing us as a people for himself he also ordained the necessary means, namely, the shedding of the guiltless blood of Christ.

Theologians refer to this eternal council as the covenant of redemption. God the Father laid a charge on the Son on behalf of his foreknown chosen people. The Son voluntarily accepted this charge, namely, that he would take up their cause and die for them upon the cross. In return, the Father promised him the salvation of all the elect, those chosen in eternity for eternal life as his people and bride.[2]

The doctrine of election cites this set purpose of God in Christ as the cause of our individual salvation. "Why is anyone a Christian?" we ask. One might answer, "Because they believed the gospel." But we go on and ask, "Why did they believe while others did not?" The issue then is this: Is it because of something in the Christian that is more spiritual, that is better in some way, that enables him to believe while others hear the same message and do not? The Bible says no! It is not because of anything in us, but because of something in God, namely, his own sovereign choice, his eternal election of individuals to be his own through faith in Jesus Christ. This is good news to all who believe, for here is the foundation of your salvation—not something in you, who are so weak and changing, so mixed in your affections, so inconstant in your faith—it is the foundation of God's sovereign choice from eternity past. "He chose us in Christ before the foundation of the world."

The Bible's Teaching, Not Man's

Having declared and explained this doctrine that is so plainly stated in our text, I want to work it out in terms of common questions and misapprehensions. The first point in this regard is that election is the Bible's teaching and not man's.

This is a necessary statement because so many people consider this doctrine to be a human invention. Many point to Calvin, whose name is given to a theological position that strongly affirms this doctrine, namely, Calvinism. Yet how wrong it is to assign this teaching to this man. For one thing, the doctrine has a long theological lineage that goes back far before Calvin and the sixteenth-century Reformation. Augustine, the great fourth-century theologian and bishop, emphasized God's sovereign election fervently. Indeed, if you read Augustine on these matters, you may conclude that he must be a Calvinist, until you realize that he lived over a millennium before the great Genevan Reformer. All through church history a great many teachers have not only embraced but also insisted on this doctrine, and in many centuries it was the strong majority view.

But what matters is not what theologians have believed, although it is helpful to realize church history's strong endorsement. What matters is what the Bible teaches. As Christians we are bound and obliged before God to accept what is plainly taught in God's holy Word, and upon inspection we will find that Scripture repeatedly and clearly and forcefully sets forth the doctrine of election.

Our verse alone makes this point. Paul's meaning, if difficult to accept, is unavoidable. Salvation history begins with God choosing believers in Christ before creation. In Romans 9:10, Paul uses the example of Jacob and Esau to show that before they were even born God had chosen one and rejected the other, and on what principle? Romans 9:11 tells us it was because of "God's purpose in election." We are going to look at that chapter more closely in our study of Ephesians 1:5, but there are numerous other examples from the New Testament.

One compelling example is found in Acts 13:48. There, Luke is recounting Paul's preaching at Pisidian Antioch, and in passing he observes, "And as many as were appointed to eternal life believed." Likewise, Peter teaches election, addressing his first epistle "to those who are elect" (1 Peter 1:1), and in his second epistle urging his readers to "make your calling and election sure" (2 Peter 1:10).

What about Jesus? Did he have anything to say about election? In John 15:16, he made one of the plainest statements of election, saying, "You did not choose me, but I chose you." If we think back to the disciples' selection, we find that was true. Jesus sovereignly picked them when he might easily have chosen others. It was his choosing that decided their discipleship. Jesus also spoke of the eternal security that goes with

45

divine election: "All that the Father gives me will come to me, and whoever comes to me I will never cast out. . . . And this is the will of him who sent me, that I should lose nothing of all that he has given me, but raise it up on the last day" (John 6:37–39). Jesus went on to add, "No one can come to me unless it is granted him by the Father" (John 6:65). Jesus explicitly directs his mission toward not merely the world at large but those who were given to him by the Father and who therefore come to him and are saved.

Not surprisingly, God's sovereignty in salvation is not restricted to the New Testament. In Isaiah 46:9–10, God says:

> I am God, and there is none like me,
> declaring the end from the beginning
>   and from ancient times things not yet done,
> saying "My counsel shall stand,
>   and I will accomplish all my purpose."

In the time of the exodus, Moses explained God's election of Israel with the same emphasis that Paul places on free and sovereign grace: "It was not because you were more in number than any other people that the LORD set his love on you and chose you, for you were the fewest of all peoples, but it is because the LORD loves you and is keeping the oath that he swore to your fathers" (Deut. 7:7–8).

If you are wrestling with this doctrine of election, the first question you should ask is this one: Is it taught by the Bible? The question is not yet whether you understand it or whether you like it. The question is, Does God teach it in Scripture? If he does, and this brief survey shows that he does, then your obedience to him requires you to receive it. Through the obedience of your mind you can expect God to lead you into understanding and rejoicing for what is often hard to accept at first.

Sometimes people ask me what it means to be Reformed in matters of theology. I always answer that being Reformed means that I believe not what I think should be true, not what I wish were true, but I believe what the Bible teaches is true. This is what the term *Reformed* means, namely, re-formed according to the Word of God. By that definition I am not Reformed because I believe election; rather, I believe in election because I am Reformed, that is, because I submit my reasoning to the higher authority of Scripture.

Election is the Bible's teaching and not man's—and this is the very reason people often find it so hard to accept. It cuts across the grain of the humanistic teaching in which we are so steeped; it offends the wisdom of this world; it puts to death the human pride so native to our flesh.

HUMILITY, NOT PRIDE

That leads us into the next point, because people wrongly complain that election leads to pride. People say that if I believe I am chosen by God, I must think I am somehow special and superior. But election promotes humility and not pride.

The reason for this is that election does not ascribe salvation to any merit in the Christian but rather fully embraces the biblical teaching of our depravity. It says that unless salvation is wholly of God, then I could not be saved, so great is my sin and enmity to the things of God. Arthur W. Pink explains:

> The truth of God's sovereignty . . . removes every ground for human boasting and instills the spirit of humility in its stead. It declares that salvation is of the Lord—of the Lord in its origination, in its operation, and in its consummation. . . . It tells us we are "born, not of the will of the flesh, nor of the will of man, but of God" (Jn. 1:13). And all this is most humbling to

47

the heart of man, who wants to contribute something to the price of his redemption and do that which will afford ground for boasting and self-satisfaction.[3]

Where is the ground for human boasting, when we realize that our salvation is in spite of our utter unworthiness and because of God's sovereign and amazing grace? Indeed, this is our great need—to have our pride and self-reliance laid low. And it is precisely this doctrine of sovereign election that humbles the believer's heart. Paul spells out the great humbling truth in Titus 3:3–5: "For we ourselves were once foolish, disobedient, led astray, slaves to various passions and pleasures, passing our days in malice and envy, hated by others and hating one another. But when the goodness and loving kindness of God our Savior appeared, he saved us, not because of works done by us in righteousness, but according to his own mercy."

HOLINESS, NOT LICENSE

The next question that arises is whether election leads to laziness. If my salvation is caused not by my effort but by God's mercy, then what motive have I to press on with the difficult work of sanctification? In answer, the Bible emphasizes that election promotes holiness and not license.

The question reveals a gross misunderstanding of salvation as a whole. It fails to realize that holiness is the goal for which we are saved. It is God's purpose in our salvation that we should be holy. This is Paul's emphasis in Ephesians 1:4: "He chose us . . . that we should be holy and blameless before him."

This allows me to make the categorical statement that if you are not bearing evidence of holiness, if you do not even desire to be holy, you have no reason to think you are elect. When God elected sinners, he elected them to holiness, so that holiness is the particular mark of the elect. Paul writes elsewhere, "This is the will of God, your sanctification" (1 Thess. 4:3).

This is the great priority of the Christian life—not happiness, but holiness. It was for this that we were chosen and that Christ died and rose from the dead. This is what Peter means in 2 Peter 1:10, where he tells believers to "make your calling and election sure." He is not telling us to make ourselves elect, which is impossible, but rather to gain confidence in our election, a confidence that comes through holiness alone.

What a great help this understanding is in the matter of personal holiness. If I thought that my growth in holiness arose from my desire and effort, what utter hopelessness that would produce! But here I find that long before the worlds were born God elected that I would be holy. What does this mean but that I *will be* holy; if I am in Christ I can be sure of it. Knowing that this is my destiny as a Christian, I find courage to embrace it, to become what I am meant to be, and I am emboldened to a more active faith.

D. Martyn Lloyd-Jones explains:

> Because we have been chosen to holiness we must and will become holy. . . . According to Paul we are not chosen with the possibility of holiness, but to the realization of holiness. . . . Being "chosen" and being "holy" are inseparable. . . . God, who has chosen you to holiness, will make you holy; and if the preaching of the gospel does not do so, God has other means and methods. He may strike you down with illness, He may ruin your business. God will make you holy because He has chosen you unto holiness.[4]

That being the case, let us busy ourselves in obeying this gracious but uncompromising God, who elected us to be holy.

Have you ever seen members of royalty on television or perhaps at some official event? Have you noticed the ease with which they carry themselves? It is easy for princes to learn a royal bearing. There is no difficulty at all in getting a princess to walk with grace and charm. Once they have realized who and what they are, they catch on with very little training. So also with holiness for God's elect. Once we realize that we are saints, that God has chosen us for holiness, that ours is a destiny in the light of glory, then holiness becomes no great matter or difficulty. In just this way, election promotes and greatly helps the cause of holiness.

Assurance, Not Presumption

The next point follows from what we have said, but it is important for us to consider it directly. Election, we have seen, is the Bible's teaching and not man's. It promotes humility and not pride, holiness and not license. Furthermore, and herein lies much of the importance of this doctrine, election promotes assurance of salvation but not presumption.

The difference between a right assurance of salvation and a dangerous presumption is vital to understand and clearly explained in the Bible. The Bible establishes salvation on the fulfillment of a definite condition, namely, saving faith in Jesus Christ. In an earlier chapter we defined saving faith as the combination of knowledge and belief and commitment. A person is saved only by understanding the gospel, believing it as true, then committing his or her life to Jesus as he is presented in that gospel. Thinking you are saved apart from this—whether because of good works, or religious observance, or baptism, or church membership, or an experience you had long ago at a revival, a decision you once made but no longer confirm— claiming salvation on any such grounds apart from a present saving faith in Jesus Christ is sheer presumption. It is perilous to the soul and threatens an eternity of hell to those who presume upon salvation without a saving relationship with Jesus. Election, like salvation, is only in Christ.

Where, then, is security and assurance? The answer is in Christ. We have assurance of salvation as we believe in Christ. And here is where the doctrine of election so greatly helps, because it tells us that if we can say to God that we trust in Jesus, then God tells us our faith is grounded on the solid rock of his eternal election. We are not saved by believing we are elect; rather we believe we are elect because we have faith in Christ. And having been saved through faith, God comforts us of our security in his strong hands. Election gives assurance not to unbelief but to the weakness of our saving faith, and in this it is of the greatest value to a Christian.

How many Christians lack the joy that ought to be theirs because they lack assurance? How many stumble on in weakness, burdened with doubts that would be erased if only they knew their salvation rested not in themselves but in God? Election speaks peace to trembling souls, as in this statement from the pen of B. B. Warfield:

> O weak and trembling soul, can you not find, not courage merely, but certitude in this? What matters your weakness? Your salvation rests not on it, but on God's strength. He loves you; He determined to save you; He sent His Son to save you; He has come to do it: He has done it. You are saved: it cannot fail, unless God's set purpose can fail; unless Christ's power to save can fail; unless His promises of love can fail.[5]

A sermon that helped me to grasp this assurance was preached long ago by Charles Haddon Spurgeon. The title was "Songs in the Night," and he preached it from Job 35:10, which describes God as "my Maker, who gives songs in the night." Spurgeon dwells on the darkness in which so many spiritually live, arguing the importance of gospel assurance to Christian joy. He points out that when we doubt, when we tremble for our salvation, we should turn our minds to God's saving works and promises, which come to us as songs in the night. "Let us begin," Spurgeon says, "with what God did for us in past times."

> When you yourself are low, it is well to sing of the Fountainhead of mercy; of that blessed decree that ordained you to eternal life. . . . I tell you, believer, if you can go back to the years of eternity; if you can in your mind run back to that period before the everlasting hills were fashioned, or the fountains of the great deep were scooped out; and if you can see your God inscribing your name in His eternal book—if you can see in His loving heart eternal thoughts of love to you, you will find this a charming means of giving you songs in the night. No songs [compare with] those which come from electing love. . . . In our darker hours it is our joy to sing: "Sons we are through God's election, who in Jesus Christ believe; By eternal destination, sovereign grace we now receive."[6]

GLORY TO GOD ALONE

How appropriate that the assurance that comes through this doctrine of election should be expressed in terms of singing, because ultimately it leads us in praise of God. This is the last point I want to make concerning election, that *election promotes glory to God alone and not to man.*

I began this chapter by pointing out the great importance of a deep foundation to the stability of a tall building. Let me now add that such a foundation is only as strong as its weak-

est point. If all is secure except one portion, which cannot bear
the weight and stress assigned to it, the whole edifice is doomed
to fall. This is why it is so vital that God's eternal work in our
salvation—a project higher and grander than any devised in
the minds of men—rests wholly on him alone, on God who
alone can bear the demands of our justification and our sanctification and ultimately of our final glorification in heaven.
If at any point these rest on us, on our character or our con-
stancy, on our desire or our performance, then the whole
tower is doomed to come crashing down. In contrast, as Paul
writes elsewhere, "God's firm foundation stands, bearing this
seal: 'The Lord knows those who are his'" (2 Tim. 2:19). Writing on that text, Calvin says:

> All that is given us is because God has chosen us before
> the world began; because He loved us in our Lord Je-
> sus Christ before we could do either good or evil . . .
> [Paul] sets this foundation of God against whatsoever
> virtue may be found in man: he sets this sureness of
> which he speaks against this frail state of ours. . . . If
> we find no certainty in things on earth, we must know
> that our salvation rests upon God, and that He holds
> it in such a manner that it can never vanish away. This
> is a happy consideration.[7]

All that being true—this being the foundation of our security—you see how election leads us to praise not ourselves,
not other men and women, but God alone. As Jonah 2:9 says,
"Salvation belongs to the LORD," and therefore all our praise
belongs to him.

This is how we cause our hearts to lift up in praise to God,
by reflecting on his sovereign grace. We find this modeled in
the psalms. Psalm 28:8 says, "The LORD is the strength of his
people; he is the saving refuge." Psalm 62:6 adds, "He only is

my rock and my salvation, my fortress; I shall not be shaken."
Psalm 59:16–17 completes the progression:

> But I will sing of your strength;
>> I will sing aloud of your steadfast love in the
>>> morning.
> For you have been to me a fortress
> . . . .
> O my Strength, I sing praise to you.

Can you fit those words into your mouth? Are you willing
to admit that in you there is no reason for hope, that there is
nothing in you that marks you out as different from the great
mass of unbelieving humanity? Do you agree that only if there
is such grace in God, only if God should choose you despite
your sin, with nothing of your own to commend you, before
creation and in Christ and all to the praise of his glory alone—
do you agree that it is only by this electing grace that you could
possibly be saved? If you cannot, if you recoil from the sovereign and electing grace of God, then on what are you relying?
Must you not necessarily be cherishing some merit of your own,
some strength of your own, something in you that will win you
through to heaven? There is no peace in that, and the Bible
offers you neither hope nor assurance nor joy in such a faith.

"He chose us in him before the foundation of the world,
that we should be holy and blameless before him." Those are the
words that give us assurance of God's blessing now and forever
and that put praises to God in our mouths. As one hymnist wrote,

> *Since grace is the source of the life that is*
>> *mine,*
> *And faith is a gift from on high—*
> *I'll boast in my Savior, all merit decline,*
> *And glorify God 'til I die.*[8]

5

PREDESTINED AS SONS

Ephesians 1:5

In love he predestined us for adoption through
Jesus Christ, according to the purpose of his will.
—Ephesians 1:5

In an earlier study we observed that the hymn of praise that begins Ephesians takes the form of one long sentence, running from verse 3 to verse 14. This is a departure from the conventions of Greek style, and it creates occasional problems in translation. For example, how should we take the words *in love* at the end of Ephesians 1:4? "In love" may modify what comes before it, so that our holiness should be characterized by love. In that case, it would read, "He chose us . . . that we should be holy and blameless before him in love." Or it could modify what comes after, so that love is the reason for God's predestination: "In love he predestined us."

From the grammar alone there is no way to choose between the two options, so we have to decide on other grounds. I agree with most English translations that the context argues for the second view. Paul's emphasis in this passage is on God the Father, so this clause more likely refers to him. Paul's special concern is the love of the Father as the fount of every blessing in Christ. Paul's placement of this phrase is awkward, but that suggests an emphasis on this point, namely, that salvation ultimately starts in the love of God. His concern is the same as that of the apostle John, when he wrote, "So we have come to know and to believe the love that God has for us" (1 John 4:16).

What a difference it makes, what peace and joy it brings, to realize that our salvation depends on God's love for us, for God's love is eternal, unchanging, and almighty. J. I. Packer writes, "Whereas human love . . . cannot ensure that what is desired for the beloved will actually happen . . . divine love is a function of omnipotence, and has at its heart an almighty purpose to bless which cannot be thwarted."[1]

PREDESTINATION

This is Paul's point in Ephesians 1:5, that in his love—his infinite and eternal and omnipotent love—God "predestined us for adoption through Jesus Christ." Predestination means that God determined something in advance, in this case that we should be children and heirs in his family. This verse complements the one that precedes it, which spoke of God electing, or choosing, us. Ephesians 1:5 gives the reason for our election, namely, God's predetermined purpose for our adoption in Christ. God chose us in Christ to be holy and blameless because he had predestined us to be his sons.

Many people find the idea of divine predestination difficult to accept, and they labor to deny the plain meaning of texts like this. But the apostle's teaching is unambiguous; he clearly states that our spiritual blessings originate in God's eternal election (Eph. 1:4) on the basis of divine predestination. This means that God foreordained the salvation of the elect, here expressed in terms of holiness and sonship.

One way people deny this is to say that God merely predestined that there would be a holy people to be his children through faith in Christ. All that Paul means, this view says, is that this is how God organized salvation, without deciding who would partake of it. But the language of this passage refutes such reasoning. Paul does not say that God chose that there would be *a* holy people in Christ but that he chose *us* for this. Ephesians 1:5 does not say that God predestined the principle of adoption as the way of salvation but that "he predestined us," namely, Paul and the Christian readers of this letter, to be adopted into his family. God chose us to be his holy people; he predestined us to be his adopted sons.

Another denial of predestination arises from Paul's language in Romans 8:29. There, Paul writes, "For those whom he foreknew he also predestined to be conformed to the image of his Son, in order that he might be the firstborn among many brothers." Here, predestination is preceded by foreknowledge. People argue that this means that God foresees that certain people will believe and then predestines that they will be saved. What God foresees or foreknows is our faith, according to this view, so that salvation ultimately rests on our act of believing, which causes or allows God to choose us. But this nullifies the very idea of election; it renders pointless the teaching Paul is so clearly trying to convey, namely, that salvation rests on God's character and purpose. Such a teaching denies salvation by grace alone, making it instead depend on our believing, which gives us a sort of merit in God's eyes. Paul denies this very thing, writing in Titus 3:5, "He saved us, not because of works done by us in righteousness, but according to his own mercy."

On what basis did God predestine those who are saved? According to what principle? Ephesians 1:5 answers this directly. "In love he predestined us," Paul writes, "according to" . . . what? In accordance with God foreseeing our faith? No. "He predestined us . . . according to the purpose of his will." Predestination is sovereign and gratuitous; it rests not on what we are or have done but on God's "pleasure and will" (NIV).

Here is where the phrase *in love* becomes important to Paul's point. Romans 8:29 says God predestined us having foreknown us; our verse says that God predestined us "in love." These two are synonymous, for God foreknew us in the biblical sense—he loved us. We might read our passage, "Having foreloved us, he predestined us." This is what Moses explained regarding the election of Israel, in Deuteronomy 7:7–8. Why did God choose you, he asked? It was not because you were great or numerous, "but it was because the LORD loved you." Behind the mystery of divine election is the greater and majestic mystery of God's sovereign love for sinners. John Owen writes, "Election reveals the glory of God's nature which is love, for 'God is love' (1 Jn. 4:8, 9). . . . If we could look into all the treasures hidden in God's wonderful nature, we would find none to which election could be truly attributed but love."[2]

God loved us in eternity, predestined us for adoption as his sons, and therefore chose us to be holy and blameless in his sight, all in and through our Lord Jesus Christ.

PREDESTINATION AND HUMAN RESPONSIBILITY

In our last chapter I dealt with a number of misconceptions and questions concerning election. I now want to consider two main objections that are leveled against predestination. The first is that predestination rules out human will and responsibility. This makes sense to people, for if salvation is based on a decision God made before time then what people do today seems to be of no significance. Many people point out passages in the Bible that demand a response or a choice and therefore declare that predestination is impossible. Did not Joshua say to Israel, "Choose this day whom you will serve. . . . But as for me and my household, we will serve the LORD" (Josh. 24:15)? Doesn't that prove that we are saved by what we decide, rather than by what God decides?

The answer to this is that the Bible teaches both divine predestination and full human responsibility. Our theology must be able to incorporate both Ephesians 1:5 and Joshua 24:15, both the many passages that speak of God's utter sovereignty in salvation and those that declare humanity's utter responsibility before God. The best way to begin to deal with this issue, then, is to realize that the Bible vigorously teaches both.

How, then, do we reconcile the two? The answer is that we don't. Here is a place for us to practice John Calvin's excellent principle: Where the Bible makes an end of teaching, let us make an end of learning. The Bible asserts both predestination and human responsibility without reconciling them, and we must be willing to leave it at that.

One observation we might make, however, is that there is always mystery where the divine and the human meet. Think of the relationship between the human and the divine natures in Jesus Christ. We can identify both, but we cannot tell where one begins and the other ends. Jesus is both fully God and fully man at the same time. Likewise, there is full divine sovereignty in our salvation and full human responsibility to believe and obey the gospel.

But doesn't predestination make us puppets, automatically doing what God has decided long in advance? The answer to this is found by considering the picture of humankind in the Bible. Ephesians 1:5, among other verses, teaches predestination, but the same Bible plainly represents men and women as exercising genuine choice. There are a number of biblical examples. Let's take Judas Iscariot. His betrayal of our Lord was prophesied in the Book of Psalms (Ps. 41:9) and also by Jesus before it even happened. The Old Testament even predicted how many pieces of silver he would be paid (Zech. 11:12–13). But is he excused for betraying our Lord? Not at all; he is plainly condemned as responsible for his wicked deeds.

Acts 27 offers another example, where Paul's ship encounters a deadly storm. In Acts 27:24, Paul reveals that God has promised the safety of all the crew. The storm increased, and a group of men sought to escape in a lifeboat. Paul then cried out that any who departed the ship would perish (Acts 27:31). God foreordained their salvation, but to stay safe they had to remain in the ship. So it is in salvation.

The most powerful biblical example is that of our Lord Jesus Christ. Here is One whose life was not merely predestined but predicted in writing in many of its details. Yet who will call God's Son a puppet, without will and responsibility? The same is true with regard to the events surrounding his death. In Acts 2:23, the apostle Peter directly ascribes Christ's death to God's election: "This man was handed over to you by God's set purpose and foreknowledge" (NIV). But he goes directly on to assign the blame to the Jews who despised him: "You, with the help of wicked men, put him to death by nailing him to the cross" (NIV). Divine sovereignty and human responsibility stand side by side in Scripture.

It is for that reason that predestination does not argue against evangelism. People say, "If God predestines people to salvation, then why bother to preach the gospel?" The answer is that God ordains not merely the ends but also the means. He predestines some to be saved and commands us to preach the gospel to that end. If we do not preach and teach the gospel, then none will be saved. But God has ordained that they will be; he has chosen his people to be saved. So he has also ordained that we would preach and share the gospel and therefore we will, exercising our human responsibility in accordance with his sovereign will. James Montgomery Boice adds:

> Besides, it is only election that gives us any hope of success as we evangelize. If God cannot call people to faith effectively, how can we? We cannot persuade them. But if God is working, then he can work in us even if we are inept witnesses. We do not know who God's elect are, but we can find out who some of them are by telling them about Jesus. . . . We can speak to them boldly because we know that God has promised to bless his Word and will not allow it to return to him without accomplishing his purpose (Isa 55:11).[3]

IS IT FAIR?

Another objection against predestination has to do with fairness. People object that if Christians are saved because of God's sovereign election, then it is not fair to hold others accountable for their sin and unbelief. It is helpful to know that this objection is dealt with in the Bible. In Romans 9, Paul treats the matter of predestination. He presents the example of Jacob and Esau, reminding us that "though they were not yet born and had done nothing either good or bad . . . she [their mother, Rebecca] was told, 'The older will serve the younger.' As it is written, 'Jacob I loved, but Esau I hated' " (Rom. 9:11–13). Paul then rhetorically presents this objection based on fairness: "What shall we say then? Is there injustice on God's part?" His reply is powerful and informative: "By no means! For he says to Moses, 'I will have mercy on whom I have mercy, and I will have compassion on whom I have compassion' " (Rom. 9:14–15).

Paul's point is that when we consider the salvation of sinners, justice is the wrong category. Justice offers only condemnation: "For all have sinned and fall short of the glory of God" (Rom. 3:23). It is not as if God looked down on a neutral humanity, deciding to make some believe and others reject him. Rather, he looked upon a humanity already guilty in sin and unbelief. This is why election is in Christ. It is joined with God's intention to send his Son to die for the sins of the elect. God predestines some sinful rebels to be saved, passing by other sinful rebels to allow them to continue their chosen hell-bound course. The only reason anyone is saved is because of God's mercy, for as Paul adds, "It depends not on human will or exertion, but on God, who has mercy" (Rom. 9:16).

God shows his mercy in the election of some to be saved. But God intends to be glorified not just in mercy but in all his attributes. He also is just, and he will show his justice, to the praise of his name, in the judgment of sinners who willfully rebel against him. God is sovereign. And he displays his sovereignty by choosing some and passing over others. God is God, and he will be sovereign even in salvation. Jonathan Edwards explains, "It is the will of God to manifest his sovereignty. And his sovereignty, like his other attributes, is manifested in the exercise of it. He glorifies his power in the exercise of his power. He glorifies his mercy in the exercise of his mercy. So he glorifies his sovereignty in the exercise of his sovereignty."[4]

Predestination is not unjust, because everyone in hell will have been condemned for their own choice to sin and reject God. A. W. Tozer rightly said, "There will be only one text in hell, and it may be cut against the great walls of that terrible place—'True and righteous are thy judgments, O Lord!' "[5] But heaven's song will be "Amazing grace—how sweet the sound—that saved a wretch like me!"[6] Boice therefore writes, "It is not justice we want from God; it is grace. And grace cannot be commanded. It must flow to us from God's sovereign purposes decreed before the foundation of the world, or it must not come at all."[7]

ADOPTION AS SONS

All through Ephesians we will be asking the question, What is a Christian? This is one of Paul's emphases in this book, and Ephesians 1:5 presents another answer. Ephesians 1:1 told us that Christians are "saints who are . . . faithful in Christ Jesus." Here, we find that a Christian is a child of God: "He predestined us for adoption."

The Bible speaks of Christians as God's children in at least three ways. First, Christians are born again so as to partake of God's nature; we are spiritual members of his family, with Jesus as firstborn through the resurrection. This idea is prominent in John's writings, although we will hear of it from Paul. Second, Christians are adopted by God to receive the privileges of being his sons. Third, as children of God we are heirs of God's eternal blessings alongside of Jesus Christ. In Ephesians 1:5 it is the second of these that is mainly in view.

The idea of salvation as adoption seems to be a distinctively Pauline expression, and since he uses it only in letters written to or from Rome, it seems that he draws this concept from the example of Roman civil law. Adoption was not uncommon in Roman society, and adopted children enjoyed the same full rights as natural-born children. Adoption generally involved the taking of sons, often to carry on a family line as heir. This is why we should maintain a male distinction in the matter of adoption. Just as all Christians are brides of Christ, male and female, so also are all adopted as sons of God.

The Christian writer Lew Wallace wrote *Ben Hur* about a Jewish prince who was taken as a slave by the Romans. Later he saved the life of a Roman consul, ultimately being adopted as his son and receiving his signet ring of power and authority. That rise from slave to royal heir well depicts our elevation from shameful sinners to those made holy in Christ and thus adopted as God's sons.

Adoption involved an elaborate legal procedure, culminating with the father presenting his new son before the Roman magistrate. It effected a radical change, severing the old family ties, and in the same way Christians are separated by adoption out from sin and from the world. Roman adoption was so radical a separation that all past debts and obligations were wiped out; so also does God separate us from our debt and from our allegiance in service to sin.

Adoption makes us full members of God's family, not second-class children. It provides us all the privileges of sonship, with obligations as well. What are these privileges? First, we have a relationship with God as our Father; we come to him familiarly, calling him Father, with open access to his presence. Second, we have God's care and provision, materially and spiritually through the Holy Spirit. Third, we have the privilege of God's fatherly discipline as he works in us for a harvest of righteousness and peace. Fourth, we become heirs of all our Father's goods. These privileges are all reflected in a modern-day adoption certificate, one of which I saw reads this way: "Said ADOPTEE shall have all rights of a child and be heir of the adopting parents and shall be subject to duties of such child. Said ADOPTEE shall hereafter be known as . . . " and a space is given for a new name to be assigned. So it is with our adoption into God's family. With these privileges come responsibilities; they include bearing God's name nobly in this world, doing his will, obeying him as our Father and sovereign Lord, defending and advancing the cause of his household and reign.

The final privilege we receive in adoption is acceptance as beloved brothers with Jesus Christ. By nature we were a disgrace before God, having nothing in common with God's divine Son. But in his love, God predestined us for adoption, and therefore Jesus took up our flesh to make us holy and without blemish, as Ephesians 1:4 says, and thereby made us fit to be his brothers. He united himself with us in the incarnation in order to make atonement for our sins (Heb. 2:17), and we are spiritually joined with him through faith. Thus he presents us before God on the basis of the holiness he provides. Hebrews 2:11–13 declares, "For he who sanctifies and those who are sanctified all have one origin [or "are of the same family," NIV]. That is why he is not ashamed to call them brothers, saying, 'I will tell of your name to my brothers . . . . Behold, I and the children God has given me.' " He is our elder brother, so that our adoption is, as Paul emphasizes, "through Jesus Christ."

Sinclair B. Ferguson draws out three vital implications of our adoption. The first is that "adoption is not a change in nature, but a change in status." He writes, "If we think of adoption as based on anything we have done, or on what we are, then we will jeopardize our assurance of God's fatherly relation to us. Adoption is, instead, a *declaration God makes about us.* It is irreversible, dependent entirely on his gracious choice." Second, he adds, "adoption into a new family produces conflict with the old family." We should not be surprised when Satan and the sinful world seek to win back our allegiance through lies and temptations. Third, "adoption is incomplete in this world." Our status is now finalized, but not our experience of sonship. Paul writes in Romans 8:19 that creation itself "waits with eager longing for the revealing of the sons of God." We ourselves long for and labor toward full conformity to Jesus Christ, which Paul describes as "the freedom of the glory of the children of God" (Rom. 8:21).[8]

LOVE SO AMAZING

In the church where I formerly served, there was a Christian couple who adopted a baby girl. They had tried unsuccessfully for many years to give birth to a child, and with much prayer they finally concluded that God would have them adopt. They were driven by a great love within themselves that longed for a child, and they were motivated by the picture of God's love presented in this verse. It was in love that they pursued adoption; love was the fount and source of all that would transpire in this child's adoption, just as it is in God's adoption of us into his family.

Having learned from another family's experience of adopting a child from Russia, this couple made the applications, satisfied the various requirements, and finally received a picture of the child who could be their own. All they had was a photograph, but they poured their love into the child they only knew this way, giving her a name, praying for her, and starting to buy the things she would need as a baby in their home.

Here was this orphan child in a faraway land, without parents and oblivious to this great love moving in the hearts of these Christians. They were planning her adoption and storing up blessings. I think of them gazing with love into just a picture of their child, and realize that this only dimly reflects God's loving foreknowledge of us. Like this, God set his love on us from afar and predestined our adoption as his sons.

The time came when the husband and wife departed for Russia. There were problems with their travel, but finally, they arrived in a strange land where they would spend ten days seeking their child. They met with medical officials who suggested frightening reports of problems with the baby's health and development. At one point they had to fend off another family's attempt to get their baby. After days of persisting and working through the system they finally came before a Russian court to plead their fitness to take this baby girl. So many obstacles, so much expense, so many difficulties and problems—what brought them through it all? It was their great love for this child, whom they had known from afar but had named and cherished, and for whom they had stored up rich blessings. Finally, love won through and with great joy that baby came home as their daughter, to be lavished with their favor and to enter into the joy of their home.

Think, then, of what it took for God's love to win through in your adoption. God faced a greater barrier than distance or bureaucracy; he faced the obstacle of your sin, against which stood his holy nature. But what lengths he pursued that you might be beloved as his child! He sent his natural and divine Son into this world to take up our infirmities, to enter into the misery and humiliation of this fallen age, to live the life we should have lived, holy and blameless before God. Having fulfilled all righteousness he offered himself up for judgment in our place. Peter writes, "Christ also suffered once for sins, the righteous for the unrighteous, that he might bring us to God" (1 Peter 3:18). What is the measure of God's love for you but the outstretched arms of Jesus Christ upon the wooden beams of his cross? What is the price God's love will pay to take away your sin, but the precious blood of Jesus, "the Lamb that was slain from the creation of the world" (Rev. 13:8 NIV).

That is the pursuing love of God that crosses oceans of time and in almighty grace takes you as his precious child and son. Surely like the father in Jesus' parable of the prodigal son, he will see you coming from afar, race out to meet you as you come along the way, bath you with kisses and tears, drape on your shoulders a robe of righteousness, and call out, "My son, my son!"

"In love he predestined us for adoption through Jesus Christ, according to the purpose of his will." How else can we respond but to cry out to him with love in return, calling him Father and taking our place with joy as sons of God? As the hymnist says, so we sing:

Your saving love has triumphed Lord,
Your grace has conquered me.
Now pardoned, cleansed, redeemed, restored,
I lift my heart in worship, Lord,
Your yielded child to be.[9]

6

THE GLORY OF
HIS GRACE

Ephesians 1:6

*To the praise of his glorious grace, with which
he has blessed us in the Beloved.*
—Ephesians 1:6

One of the exciting things about studying the Bible is
the new heights to which it constantly lifts us. On our
own we dwell on the level of the mundane, if not the ignoble,
but the Bible speaks to us of grander and greater things. Already we have experienced this in our studies of Ephesians.
Ephesians 1:3 spoke of unseen heavenly realms in which we
have great spiritual blessings in Christ. Paul wants us to take
possession of these spiritual treasures by faith. Ephesians 1:4
then told of God's sovereign election, which has the aston-

ishing goal that we should be "holy and blameless." We would be glad to settle for so much less than that, for a little peace and prosperity, but the Bible directs our gaze upward to the infinitely higher destiny of holiness. Ephesians 1:5 takes us still higher, saying that God all along has destined us to be adopted as his sons. That is a privilege for which words are barely available and which in our present experience we hardly grasp. The best gauge of this high station is to consider our Lord Jesus' relationship to the Father and to realize that we are called into the same blessed relationship.

As if this were not enough, Ephesians 1:6 brings before us a higher purpose yet. Paul is taking us ever upward, first to holiness and then to our adoption. But high above these great peaks looms a greater summit yet, namely, God's purpose to manifest and display in us the "praise of his glorious grace, with which he has blessed us in the Beloved." This is the Bible's way of sanctification, to lift our hearts and minds up from the things of earth to the glories of heaven. Paul says this in Colossians 3:1–2, "If then you have been raised with Christ, seek the things that are above, where Christ is, seated at the right hand of God. Set your minds on things that are above, not on things that are on earth."

GLORIOUS GRACE

The next verse in our study of Ephesians concludes the first section in this grand hymn of praise to God. Ephesians 1:4–6 tell us that salvation begins in the sovereign grace of God and comes to its conclusion in the resplendent glory of God. These are two great principles of the Protestant Reformation, and they go together inseparably: *sola gratia*, salvation by grace alone, and *soli deo gloria*, glory to God alone. In them the whole of the Christian religion is contained. Paul summed this all up in the great doxology of Romans 11:36, "For from him and through him and to him are all things. To him be glory forever. Amen."

In Ephesians 1:6, Paul directs us to the glory of God in salvation by making three points. First, he reminds us that God's grace is glorious. Second, he tells us that God's grace comes to us only through Jesus Christ, the Beloved of God. Finally, he points out that salvation is directed toward the praise of this glorious grace that is in Christ.

The first point is that God's grace is glorious. This seems like an obvious statement; after all, everything about God is glorious, such as his justice and power and goodness. But Paul's point is that it is particularly God's grace, especially God's grace, that will glorify God at the end of the ages. I want to consider the glory of God's grace from three perspectives, namely, in terms of what grace reveals about God, of the difficulty of what grace attempts and achieves, and finally of the incomparable effects that are produced by God's glorious grace.

What grace reveals about God. God's grace is glorious in what it reveals to us about him. Recently a number of philanthropists have received a great deal of public attention. A new Center for the Performing Arts was built in Philadelphia, named for the man who gave the most money to the project. This man was praised in the media for giving so many millions to the arts and also for having funded the building of hospitals. He is a great philanthropist, that is, a lover of his fellow man. For this he is glorified, and future generations will know from these buildings that while our generation as a whole pursued only the selfish use of money, this man thought of the betterment of others. Christians ought to praise this and have gratitude for the advancement of the arts and of medicine.

Another example is the computer mogul Bill Gates, who with his wife has been in the news for giving tens of billions for philanthropy. Their picture was on the cover of a national magazine for this. Again, Christians should be the first to respond with approval. This man worked hard, had a vision, and now is giving back vast sums of his wealth for the betterment of humankind. He is glorified for his generosity, and rightly so.

But great as these examples of philanthropy are, they are nothing when compared with the love that flows from the grace of God. Consider, for instance, that none of these tycoons impoverished themselves. They gave away money they never could have spent. What they did was good and worthy of our praise, but how much more glorious is God in his abounding grace! God gave not excess riches but his one and only Son for us. Furthermore, these worldly philanthropists gave to their fellow beings, to those who by rights they ought to love and care for. But God gave his grace to those who were his enemies, those who had sinned against him and victimized him with intentional malice. Paul put it this way: "God shows his love for us in that while we were still sinners, Christ died for us" (Rom. 5:8). Consider as well the boundless love of Jesus. "For you know the grace of our Lord Jesus Christ," Paul says, "that though he was rich, yet for your sake he became poor, so that you by his poverty might become rich" (2 Cor. 8:9).

These human benefactors gave generously but not sacrificially. But God gave the very best that he had for sinners and rebels, and Jesus Christ offered his precious blood for our redemption. This is God's grace in its glory, and against this blazing sun all other grace, all other glory, pales into dimness.

The Bible presents many scenes that reveal God's love for his people. One great picture comes from the prophet Hosea, who lived in a time of widespread sin and apostasy. God told the prophet to love and marry a faithless woman to symbolize God's relationship with Israel. Hosea thus married Gomer, had three children by her, and gave her his heart. But then Gomer left him to chase after her lovers. God used this not only to show how Israel had forsaken him but also to reveal his great love for his people.

As Gomer ran off into adultery, God had Hosea provide for her needs, never failing in his love. Gomer was passed from lover to lover, until she finally was brought naked in the town square to be sold as a slave. Into that scene came her husband, Hosea. God said to him, "Go again, love a woman who is loved by another man and is an adulteress, even as the LORD loves the children of Israel" (Hos. 3:1). Hosea went forth and put down the purchase price for the wife who had betrayed and humiliated him, foreshadowing our ransom by the blood of Christ. "And I said to her," Hosea recounts, "'You must dwell as mine for many days. You shall not play the whore, or belong to another man; so will I also be to you'" (Hos. 3:3). Reflecting on this scene, God declares to us, "I will betroth you to me forever. I will betroth you to me in righteousness and in justice, in steadfast love and in mercy" (Hos. 2:19).

What kind of love is that? It is the love of heaven, the love of God, the love by which sinners like us can hope to be saved. It is a love that is glorious in abounding grace, love that calls us to faith and devotion in return.

That kind of grace is what we are called to display before the world. Grace is what is most attractive about Christianity, what sets it apart from every other religion. Nothing is more unappealing and out of sync with biblical Christianity than shrill judgmentalism or bitter divisiveness. And nothing so glorifies God in this world than the grace and forgiveness displayed by Christians. It is natural for us to sue people who do us wrong, to return harsh words with a poisoned response, to respond in anger when our rights are trampled, to condemn and reject those who hurt us, but it glorifies God's grace when instead we respond with his love. Christianity is a religion of the grace that comes from God. God's grace is glorious in revealing God's love for humankind, even for sinners, and when grace is displayed in our lives it makes us as lights shining in the darkness of the world.

The difficulty of what grace does. God's grace is glorious not only in revealing God's love but also in terms of the difficulty of what it attempts and achieves. In the Olympic games there are a number of sports in which you can get more points according to the difficulty level. But when it comes to difficulty, it is God's grace that earns the gold medal.

God receives glory for doing things that are difficult beyond our comprehension. He created the universe from nothing, and thus the heavens declare the glory of his power. But God's grace tackles a problem far more difficult than mere creation. I mean this reverently, but there is no special wisdom in the raw display of divine power in creation. This is what a God does! The angels do not marvel at the logic of this, however magnificent is the display. But our salvation reveals a grace that is glorious in overcoming a problem of infinite difficulty, the greatest problem in all history, the problem of our sin.

Men or women are honored for doing something very difficult. In the Olympics, for instance, athletic champions are crowned with glory and honor, and some of them with great riches. This is true in other fields as well. The names of great inventors, like Benjamin Franklin and Thomas Edison, are held in great esteem for overcoming great difficulties in our ignorance. The same is true with great industrialists, like Henry Ford, who overcame serious problems of organization and production. There are explorers who overcame great difficulties of danger and prowess. Neil Armstrong will ever be glorified for being the first man to step on the moon. Researchers are held in the highest esteem for overcoming dread diseases. Jonas Salk is still revered for defeating polio, saving countless millions of lives. Imagine today the glory that would rightly go to any man or woman who discovered a cure for AIDS or cancer.

But against all these, God's grace blazes with an unsurpassable glory. In salvation God overcomes the greatest problem of all, namely, our sin. This could not be put more powerfully than the way Paul does in chapter 2 of this letter. "You were dead in the trespasses and sins . . . and were by nature children of wrath." This is our problem, a corruption in our very nature because of sin, so that only one kind of life is open to us, one bound by "the passions of our flesh," one that follows the sinful "desires of the body and the mind," which lead only to judgment and death. "But," Paul says—and here is the whole gospel—"God, being rich in mercy, because of the great love with which he loved us, even when we were dead in our trespasses, made us alive together with Christ—by grace you have been saved" (Eph. 2:1–5). This "you" of salvation describes people like us who were by nature opposed to God and were spiritually dead, but God by his grace brought us to new life. We will glorify someone who cures AIDS or cancer or any number of other afflictions, but here is God's grace, which overcomes the fount of all these afflictions, namely, sin, and gives us triumph even over death. It is grace that cries, "O death, where is your victory? O death, where is your sting?" (1 Cor. 15:55).

But even this is not the greatest difficulty surmounted by God's grace. Greater yet is the problem within God that must be overcome for us to be saved. In our salvation, God overcomes the infinite weight of his holy judgment; God's changeless and holy character stands against the salvation of sinners, and God's grace is glorified in finding a way. Here is the wisdom, here is the victory, into which even angels long to look (1 Peter 1:12), that God may remain just and yet justify sinners through faith in Jesus Christ.

God's grace in Christ solves the problem within God, reconciling his justice with his mercy at the cross. And it goes on to solve the problem within us: unbelief, sin, rebellion to God. There is nothing more difficult in this world than turning a hardened sinner's heart to God. But God's grace does it through the power of the Holy Spirit. And it is precisely because grace is difficult—in forgiveness, in love for those who hurt us—that it is so glorious. It is too hard to forgive, too hard to repent of sin, you say. But it is precisely by giving us power through the Spirit to do what is so hard that God is glorified through our lives. Where all else has failed, God's grace melts our hearts, fills us with his love, and thereby glorifies itself before the world.

The effects that God's grace produces. God's grace is glorious in the incomparable effects it brings. This is what history will reveal in the end. Isaiah prophesied:

> The wolf shall dwell with the lamb,
>> and the leopard shall lie down with the young
>>> goat,
> and the calf and the lion and the fattened calf to-
>> gether;
>> and a little child shall lead them.
> . . . .
> They shall not hurt or destroy
>> in all my holy mountain;
> for the earth shall be full of the knowledge of the
>> LORD
>> as the waters cover the sea. (Isa. 11:6–9)

The result of grace is peace, divine peace, peace like a river flowing from the glorious grace of God. God's grace is glorified even now by the peace it brings to troubled hearts through faith in Christ.

The transforming power of God's grace will be glorified in the end by not only repairing what was broken in the fall but also advancing it to glory. History began with the glory of cre-

76

ation, which then fell into shame and ruin through the entry of sin. But God's grace will transform this very world into a realm of heavenly glory, the redeemed City of God, "having the glory of God, its radiance like a most rare jewel, like a jasper, clear as crystal" (Rev. 21:11). What will be true of the church and the regenerated universe will be equally true of us as glorified individuals. Jesus said, "Then the righteous will shine like the sun in the kingdom of their Father" (Matt. 13:43).

God's grace is glorious—glorious in revealing God's great love, glorious in the difficulty of what it attempts and attains, glorious in the results it effects—all to the praise of God the Father forever.

GRACE IN THE BELOVED

The passage that Ephesians 1:6 concludes is focused on the grace of God the Father. Nonetheless, Paul emphasizes the centrality of Jesus Christ in all our salvation. We have seen this all through this letter; we are only now in the sixth verse, but it contains the seventh explicit reference to Christ. Christians are "saints" and the "faithful in Christ Jesus"; our spiritual blessings are all "in Christ"; our election was "in him," and we are adopted "through Jesus Christ." Now, as he writes of the glory of God's grace, Paul is unwilling to allow the slightest separation or confusion about the centrality of Christ. Here he refers to Jesus as "the Beloved."

There is a play on words here that does not come through in the English versions. Paul employs the noun form and then the verb form of the word *grace, charis* and then *charitein*. We might replicate Paul's thought by saying, "to the praise of his glorious *grace,* which he has *begraced* us in the Beloved." Grace is something in God—there it is a noun; but it happens—it becomes a verb— only in and through Jesus Christ. By speaking of Jesus as the Beloved, Paul emphasizes that since we are in Christ through faith, God's infinite love for his Son secures his equal fatherly love for us and thus makes certain our salvation. John Calvin says, "He names [Christ] *the Beloved,* to tell us that by Him the love of God is poured out to us."[1] However unlovely we may be—and as sinners we all are spiritually unlovely—God looks on us with loving delight because we are in and a part of the Beloved.

That God's grace is available to sinners in Jesus Christ—and only in him—is the very heart of the Christian message. Harry Ironside records an episode in which this was clearly explained. The story is told by a Dr. Usher, who was a medical missionary in Turkey about a century ago. The province in which he and others were laboring received a new governor who was a staunch Muslim. At the time there was a seldom-employed law that foreigners could remain in Turkey longer than a year only if they converted to Islam, and the new governor seized this as an opportunity to strike a blow at the Christians.

Wanting to be fair, however, the governor called the missionaries to a banquet, intending to give them a chance to become Muslims before he had them expelled. He began by asking one of them how he thought a man could enter paradise. The Christian replied that through the merits of Jesus Christ our sins are forgiven. But at this the governor only scoffed: "I cannot believe that God is less righteous than I am, and I do not believe it would be righteous for God because of His friendship for another, to forgive a sinner and take him to paradise." He added that he himself would never be corrupt enough to set aside justice just because a guilty man was the friend of a friend.

During all this, Dr. Usher was seated at the governor's left hand. The question next came to him: "What would you say? How may a man be assured of entrance into paradise?" Usher replied by asking to take the situation just presented and change it slightly.

Let us think of you not merely as the governor of this province, but as the king. You have one son, the prince, whom you love tenderly. Suppose that I am the man who is in debt to the government, owing a sum so vast that I could not pay one part out of a thousand. In accordance with the law, I am cast into prison. Unworthy as I am, your son is a friend of mine: he has a deep interest in me and a real love for me. He seeks you out and says, "My father, my friend is in prison for a debt which he owes and which he cannot pay. Will you permit me to pay it all for him in order that he may go free?" And you say to him, "My son, since you are so interested and willing to pay the debt yourself, I am willing that it should be so."[2]

The prince went to the proper authorities, paid the debt in full on behalf of his friend, and then took the receipt to have him removed from the prison.

Ironside comments that even this illustration hardly does justice to what Jesus did for us.

Our Lord saw us in our great need. He paid for us, and having settled the debt He has now brought us into the royal family, washed us from every stain of sin, robed us in garments of glory and beauty, and given us a seat at the table of the King. He has taken us into favor in the Beloved so that the Father's thoughts of Christ are His thoughts of love for us who trust in Christ.[3]

When we speak of Jesus paying our debt, we refer of course to his sacrificial death on the cross. He paid for us not in money but in the coin of his precious blood. God's grace is always in Christ, and it is most fully revealed at the cross. That is why when the New Testament speaks of God's love, it nearly always goes on within a very few verses to speak also of Christ's death for us.

The cross above all else reveals the extent of God's love. But it also provides the answer to the great problem of God's holiness as it stands against our sin. We observed earlier that God's grace is glorified by accomplishing something so difficult as overcoming God's justice, and the way it does so is by the cross. Jesus satisfies God's justice by offering himself for us, and thus he has "abolished death and brought life and immortality to light through the gospel" (2 Tim. 1:10). Everything that God's grace achieves is in the Beloved, even as we learn in John 3:16, that "God so loved the world, that he gave his only Son, that whoever believes in him should not perish but have eternal life."

TO THE PRAISE OF HIS GLORIOUS GRACE

Paul tells us in this verse that God's grace is glorious and that it is in Christ. But his particular point of emphasis has to do with our salvation by grace in Christ. The purpose, he says, for which we are saved is the praise of this glorious grace of God. Our salvation, which is by grace alone, is also to God's glory alone, and this is the highest end that anything possibly could serve.

Let me briefly draw out some implications of this teaching. This passage opens a window into what is happening in this world of woe. "What is God doing?" people ask. The answer is here, that he is storing up praise to the glory of his grace in the salvation of sinners through his Son, Jesus Christ. Christians sometimes wonder, "Why did God allow sin into the world in the first place?" That is a deeper mystery than we are going to resolve, but at least a partial answer is here, namely, that in our redemption from sin he is glorified as would not otherwise be possible. Paul alludes to this great reality in Romans

11:32, the last verse before the great doxology that concludes the doctrinal portion of that letter. There, he writes, "God has consigned all to disobedience, that he may have mercy on all."

Furthermore, this verse tells us how great is the matter of our salvation, how significant it is to God. How typical it is for us to think of salvation merely in terms of our emotional and spiritual experience or merely in terms of a certain lifestyle as an end in itself. But ultimately, we find here, our salvation is not about us; God saved us with a higher motive than just our blessing. Do you realize what a solid ground this is for assurance? If we are in Christ by faith, our ultimate salvation is as certain as is God's purpose to bring glory to himself through the praise of his marvelous grace! Not only that, but by means of the fall into sin and our subsequent redemption in Christ, God has destined us, as John Stott explains, "for a higher dignity than even creation would bestow on us. He intended to 'adopt' us as his children."[4] God has so arranged salvation as to bring us the highest possible blessing and himself the highest possible praise, both of which result only through the glory of his grace.

SALVATION BY GRACE ALONE

I want to conclude by pointing out how this great verse certifies that there is no place for works in securing our salvation, since salvation is specially designed to magnify the glory of God's grace. Surely we are saved to works; having been saved we are called to a life of godliness and goodness. But this verse assures us that we cannot be saved by works. Salvation is by grace alone so that it might abound to the glory of God's grace; were our works to play any part in our being saved, then praise would be subtracted from God's grace and given to us instead.

The conclusion to the story told by Dr. Usher shows how important this is. He told the Turkish governor the story of the king's son who paid the prisoner's debt as an illustration of Christ's saving work for us. But he went on and concluded that the man thus delivered would surely live his whole life in gratitude to the prince. "You paid my debt," he would say, so "it is a joy for me to do something to show my gratitude."

The governor listened carefully, and he thought for some time. Finally, a light shone in his eye, and he said, "Oh, then, Dr. Usher, is this the reason why you have a hospital here in Turkey? Is this why you establish these schools and why you missionaries are giving your lives for our people? You are not trying to earn your way into paradise?" "No," said Dr. Usher, "our way into paradise is settled because Jesus paid the debt, and now we serve because we love Him."[5]

Beginning with that occasion, the Turkish governor, so staunch a Muslim on his arrival, changed his attitude toward Christians. He did not force the missionaries to leave and went on to show them such kindness that he ultimately was dismissed from his office because of his leniency toward Christians. The man so determined to be the Christians' enemy had been reached through the grace of God, previously unknown to him, and the missionaries had genuine hopes that he had been saved.

Our salvation is, Paul writes, "to the praise of [God's] glorious grace, with which he has blessed us in the Beloved." The fact that we, as sinners, are saved, gives praise to the glory of God's grace. And even our works, flowing out from God's love as it comes to us in Christ, redound to the praise of his grace. It is for this that we are saved, and it is for this that we now are called to live—for the glory of God's grace. And it is in this, the greatest glory in all the world, that you will find the true purpose of your life, if you will confess your sin and come to Jesus Christ in faith. As Isaac Watts resolved, having surveyed "the wondrous cross on which the Prince of glory died," "Love so amazing, so divine, demands my soul, my life, my all."[6] Amen.

7

REDEMPTION IN CHRIST

Ephesians 1:7–8

*In him we have redemption through his blood, the forgiveness
of our trespasses, according to the riches of his grace, which
he lavished upon us, in all wisdom and insight.*
—Ephesians 1:7–8

here are times in our study of the New Testament
when we will find ourselves face to face with the
very heart of the gospel. This study is one of those occasions.
We should not be surprised at this, for as we progress through
this great hymn of praise with which Paul opens Ephesians,
we now come to the point where he considers the work of Jesus Christ. Already we have considered God the Father as the
source of our salvation, but now that we turn to God's Son and

his work we focus on salvation itself, on what salvation is and how it happens.

SAVIOR FROM OUR SIN

As we pass into this new section of Paul's hymn of praise, we are passing from eternity past into history. God chose us for holiness and predestined us for adoption before there even was time. Now we read of Christ coming into the world, and Paul tells us he came to be our Redeemer, our Savior from our sins.

If you stopped people on the street and asked them about Jesus Christ, most would probably say he came as a great moral teacher and example. But the Gospels make it clear that Jesus came to save us from our sins. This was the point made by the angel to Joseph: "You shall call his name Jesus, for he will save his people from their sins" (Matt. 1:21). Jesus explained, "The Son of Man came not to be served but to serve, and to give his life as a ransom for many" (Matt. 20:28). Jesus was born into this world in order to die for the world; as Paul tells us here, Jesus came to give us "redemption through his blood, the forgiveness of our trespasses."

This brings us back to a question I have been repeatedly asking: What is a Christian? Here we have another answer—a crucial one. A Christian is a sinner who has been redeemed by the blood of Jesus Christ. If you are offended to be called a sinner, if you think that because you dress well and have good manners and present a good appearance that you are therefore different from the common lot of people, that you are free from the great problem gripping our world in misery and guilt, then this verse says that whatever else you may be, you are not a Christian. Unless you are willing to be identified as a sinner, as one of the diseased for whom Jesus came as the Great Physician, unless you agree that Jesus had to die for you to be saved, then you are not one of those for whom he came. Jesus came as a Redeemer. He offered his precious blood that we might be forgiven our sins and then have new life through him.

Sin is the great problem facing this world, especially as it makes us guilty before God. Psychologists may deny the idea of sin and guilt, saying that we cannot be held responsible because sin is the result of our genes, our environment, our parents, or something else external to us. But the Bible flatly declares that God holds us responsible for our sins. Romans 6:23 says, "The wages of sin is death." Our great need today is not therapy, not stress management, not social reform, but salvation from our sins.

Notice how significant it is that sin appears where it does in Paul's presentation of Christian salvation. So far he has spoken of God having chosen a people for holiness, predestining us to be adopted as his sons. But a barrier stands in the way of God's purpose. That is what Paul deals with next, just as it is this barrier that God addressed by sending his Son into the world. D. Martyn Lloyd-Jones writes:

> The great obstacle . . . is the obstacle of sin; sin in general and sins in particular. It is our sins that have come between us and God. . . . So before we can ever arrive at the predestined position which God has purposed for us, something has to be done about this problem of our sin and our sins. It was to perform this special and particular work that the Son of God came into this world.[1]

REDEMPTION FROM SIN

The way that Jesus dealt with the problem of sin is clearly set forth in Ephesians 1:7, namely, "redemption through his blood." Redemption is one of the great words of our faith. It is not without reason that so many of our hymns praise our Lord for this, for redemption is something to sing about, in terms of what it does for us and what it cost to him:

O for a thousand tongues to sing
My great Redeemer's praise.[2]

All hail, Redeemer, hail!
For thou hast died for me.[3]

I will sing of my Redeemer,
And his wondrous love for me:
On the cruel cross he suffered,
From the curse to set me free.[4]

Redemption is a term that is borrowed from the marketplace and involves the idea of buying something. It presupposes some kind of bondage or captivity, circumstances that afflict us but from which we are not able to free ourselves. It was the common practice in ancient warfare for conquerors to take captives to be used as slaves. However, when someone of great wealth or high station was captured, he normally was not enslaved but instead was redeemed, that is, set free after a ransom was paid. Redemption takes us from slavery to freedom, from affliction to salvation.

Redemption was an important part of the Old Testament economy. In order to keep some Israelites from falling into permanent slavery or destitution, there was a provision whereby a kinsman redeemer was obliged to pay his relative's debts, to purchase him out from slavery, and to buy back family land that had been lost (see Lev. 25:25–28). The greatest Old Testament example of redemption is God's deliverance of Israel from their bondage in Egypt in the exodus. This is how God described it to Moses: "I will deliver you from slavery to them, and I will redeem you with an outstretched arm and with great acts of judgment" (Exod. 6:6–7).

Redemption, therefore, speaks of God saving us from a situation we could never get ourselves out of, just as the Israelites would have remained in Egypt forever if God had not come to their aid. The New Testament takes this concept and applies it to the problem of our sin. Sin is our great problem, but even worse, it is a problem that we cannot solve by ourselves. We think of sin as a small thing, indulgences that do us little harm, especially if nobody seems to be hurt and if we are able to get away with them. But the Bible says that the result of sin is slavery, bondage, and crushing affliction out of which we are totally unable to escape on our own.

James Montgomery Boice observes, "There is a parallel between the ways in which a person could fall into slavery in antiquity and how a person is said to be bound by sin in the Bible."[5] First, he explains, a person might be born into slavery, and in the same way the Bible speaks of all humankind since Adam being born into sin, inheriting from his sin a sinful nature. David acknowledged this, lamenting, "Surely I was sinful at birth, sinful from the time my mother conceived me" (Ps. 51:5 NIV). Second, as we noted, a person might be enslaved as a result of military conquest. Similarly, we are mastered by sin's power over our flesh and enticed into sin by temptations. Third, one might have debts he could not pay and find himself sold into slavery. Likewise, our sin creates a debt before God's justice that we can never repay and that binds us under the curse of guilt. In all of these ways, our situation in sin is like that of a slave; included is the miserable living condition experienced by slaves, which Paul expresses by saying, "The wages of sin is death" (Rom. 6:23). He means not just death at the end of life, nor even the damnation of sinners in hell after death, but mainly the misery with which sin presently afflicts us, so that bondage to sin is a living death.

87

That is the bad news of our sin; as Jesus declared, "Everyone who commits sin is a slave to sin" (John 8:34). As slaves, we cannot live free lives. Because of our sinful nature's corrupting influence on our choices and desires, we cannot meaningfully speak of having a free will. We make choices, but our will is in bondage to sin, which is why we keep on sinning. Furthermore, we cannot relate to God in the way he intended, as beloved children, since our sin excludes us from his holy fellowship. Sin is bondage, and having been born in sin, having chosen sin on our own, having accrued a great debt of sin's guilt before God, there is nothing we can do on our own to escape this slavery and its ruin.

BOUGHT BY HIS BLOOD

That is why Paul praises God for the redemption we have in Jesus Christ. Jesus came to us as Moses came to Israel in Egypt, to deliver us from bondage. But there is a second component for us to consider in the biblical idea of redemption, namely, the payment of a ransom as the instrument of our freedom. Jesus redeemed us, Paul says, "through his blood."

This refers to Jesus' death on the cross, which the Bible identifies as a ransom to free us from our sins. Jesus said that he came "to give his life as a ransom for many" (Matt. 20:28). John Murray explains that our redemption consisted in Jesus' "substitutionary blood-shedding . . . with the end in view of thereby purchasing to himself the many on whose behalf he gave his life a ransom."[6]

The question arises, To whom did Christ pay this ransom? Many in the early church taught that he paid it to Satan, since the Bible speaks of our bondage to him. But the Bible speaks of Christ conquering the devil, not buying him off. Hebrews 2:14 says that by his death Jesus destroyed the devil and his power. It is better to think of his ransom as being paid to God's law, to release us from the law's curse on sin. This is what Paul writes in Galatians 3:13: "Christ redeemed us from the curse of the law by becoming a curse for us." Likewise, Colossians 2:14 speaks of Christ dying so as to "cancel the written code, with its regulations, that was against us and that stood opposed to us; he took it away, nailing it to the cross" (NIV).

If you have ever been summoned before an earthly court, you know what a terrifying thing it is to stand accused before the law. But this is something the Bible says is true of us all. Revelation 20:12 tells us there will be a judgment at the end of the ages when all will stand before God's throne and the books will be opened. We will all be judged by what is written in God's books, according to what we have done.

If you realize how perfectly holy God is, and what a sinner you have been and are, that is a more terrifying thought than standing before any human judge. You will realize what Paul says in Ephesians 2:3, that we are "by nature children of wrath," and what he says at the beginning of Romans (1:18), that "the wrath of God is revealed from heaven against all ungodliness and unrighteousness of men." As our verse says, we have trespasses against God's law that bring us into judgment, and we desperately need a Savior. This is what Paul declares here. Taking our sins upon himself, paying with his own blood the debt we owed to God's holy justice, Jesus redeemed us from the law's curse and condemnation. "We have," he says, "redemption through his blood, the forgiveness of our trespasses."

COMPLETE AND FULL FORGIVENESS

Forgiveness of our sin is always first and foremost in salvation. It is forgiveness that takes us from God's curse to his blessing, from rejection to acceptance. It is of the greatest importance, then, that we should understand our forgiveness in light of Christ's redeeming work.

The question may arise in your mind, for instance, as to how thorough is this forgiveness. Does it mean that all your sins are forgiven? And to what extent does God forgive you? Is he like us in that while he may want to forgive us, the pain and horror of what we have done is too strong for him to fully put away? The Bible answers all these questions emphatically. Paul says, "He forgave us all our sins" (Col. 2:13 NIV). God promises, "I will forgive their wickedness and will remember their sins no more" (Heb. 8:12 NIV). The psalmist therefore exults, "As far as the east is from the west, so far does he remove our transgressions from us" (Ps. 103:12). Christ's redeeming work completely removes all our sins forever from God's sight.

Charles Colson tells of watching a television interview with Albert Speer, Hitler's confidante and industrialist, who after World War II was stricken with a great sense of guilt for the horrors he had assisted. Of all the war criminals tried at Nuremburg, Speer was the only one to admit his guilt, for which he served twenty years in Spandau prison. In one of his books Speer commented that his guilt never could or should be forgiven and that he would forever be seeking to atone for his sins. Commenting on this, his interviewer pressed him as to whether it would ever be possible for him to be forgiven. Speer shook his head, replying, "I don't think it will be possible." Colson remarks on Speer's obvious desperation to have his guilt removed. "I wanted to write Speer," he recalls, "to tell him about Jesus and his death on the cross, about God's forgiveness. But there wasn't time. [That] interview was his last public statement; he died shortly after."[7]

The best way to be sure about your complete, full, and final forgiveness through faith in Jesus Christ is to consider the value of the ransom with which Jesus bought you from condemnation. No doubt your sin is very great. Most of us could stand to have a healthier appreciation of the extent and cost of our sin, but some of us are weighed down with sins we have committed that seem beyond redemption. Then consider the price with which you were redeemed, the precious blood of the Son of God. What debt can you have that cannot be purchased by that? Jesus has paid the price and suffered the punishment for your sin; what is there left for you to endure? God has been paid, and the debt to his justice is gone. All that is left is for you to joyfully embrace the free forgiveness of God, who out of his grace redeemed you through the blood of his beloved Son.

Paul's intention is that realizing this, understanding the completeness of our forgiveness and the inestimable price paid for us by Christ, we should respond by giving the whole of our hearts in praise to God. He tells us that our redemption is "according to the riches of [God's] grace." This is the kind of redemption that is appropriate to a God whose grace is so glorious and rich. When it comes to our redemption, we need not bring one penny, for God is rich enough in his grace to pay all that we need, and it glorifies him to save us in this way. Charles Hodge writes, "It is the overflowing abundance of unmerited love, inexhaustible in God, and freely accessible through Christ."[8]

R. Kent Hughes urges us to make a distinction here between the idea of God redeeming us *out of* the riches of his grace (which he certainly does) and the nobler idea of God redeeming us *according to* the riches of his grace. He cites a picture of John D. Rockefeller, once the richest man in the world, dressed in a top hat and waistcoat placing a dime into the hand of an impoverished child. Rockefeller gave those ten cents out of his riches, but the gift was hardly in accordance with his great resources.[9] Not so with God; his gift lavishes us with the blessings of salvation in accordance with the riches of his grace. This infinite gift is worthy of God's infinite treasures of grace, and it commends us to grateful awe in response. God's riches are the cause of our redemption; it is because of this wealth of grace in God that Christ paid so great a price for us. Likewise, our redemption is the display of God's grace and it demands the highest praise of which we are capable. The hymnist says,

> *I bless the Christ of God;*
> *I rest on love divine;*
> *And with unfalt'ring lip and heart,*
> *I call this Saviour mine.*[10]

WITH ALL WISDOM AND UNDERSTANDING

At this point Paul's thoughts begin to cascade, as they often do in this letter. The emotional drive with which he writes sometimes makes it hard to neatly analyze his thought, and the next statement is an example of this difficulty. He is extolling God's grace, which, Paul says, "he lavished upon us, in all wisdom and insight." This clause may be taken in one of two ways. It may describe Christ's redeeming work as an example of God's wisdom and insight. Or Paul may be adding this to the forgiveness of sin as a blessing we receive through Christ's redeeming work.

The language here suggests to me that Paul is commending the "wisdom and insight" of God as displayed in our redemption. In Ephesians 1:6 he extolled the glory of God's grace. Already here he has praised "the riches of [God's] grace." Now he writes of the wisdom and insight of God's grace, and this is a fitting addition for a trilogy of praise. It is the wisdom of redemption that causes angels to marvel; Christ's death on the cross is the foolishness of God that is wiser than the wisdom of people (1 Cor. 1:25). Here is a self-sacrificing love that befuddles the world's conventional wisdom and causes us to marvel at this way of salvation that is so sublime and divine. Whenever

92

we think of the blood of Jesus Christ, shed for us, we should be reminded with thanksgiving of what God declares in Isaiah 55:9: "As the heavens are higher than the earth, so are my ways higher than your ways and my thoughts than your thoughts."

But Paul may instead mean that redemption not only gives us forgiveness but also equips us with "all wisdom and insight." Wisdom deals with our broad awareness of spiritual truth, and the word used for insight or understanding speaks of spiritual discernment for dealing with actual situations. This is what happens to us when Christ redeems us and makes us his own. In the Gospels we see him walking with and instructing the disciples, and now he does the same for us by his Spirit and through the Bible. In Romans 12:2–3 Paul writes of the mind renewal that comes about through God's transforming Word. As a result of this, he says, Christians are able to "discern what is the will of God, what is good and acceptable and perfect."

This is the freedom Jesus intends for us when he redeems us from sin, and it is this we are to seek by studying and applying the teachings of the Bible. The Gospel tells us of a man who was possessed by a great multitude of demons, depicting what it means to live under the power of sin. Luke describes him as alienated from other people, dwelling among tombs, a violent and destructive man (Luke 8:26–29). Mark adds that he cried out at night and tore his skin with stones (Mark 5:5). What a picture of the bondage of our sin! But Jesus cast out the demons and redeemed the man, freeing him from his torment. Luke writes that the people who came out later to see what happened found the man "sitting at the feet of Jesus, clothed and in his right mind" (Luke 8:35). What a true picture of salvation, of the freedom into which Jesus redeems us. Jesus brings us to himself, clothes us in his righteousness, and blesses us with "wisdom and insight," so that restored to our right mind we might go on to do his will.

Redeeming Love

In the previous chapter I mentioned the story of the prophet Hosea as an example of the glory of God's grace as it reveals his great love. God had Hosea marry Gomer, a woman who proved to be unfaithful. Yet all the while, as she pursued her lovers and descended further into sin, Hosea remained steadfast in his love for her. That story comes to its climax in a scene that illustrates Christ redeeming us from our sin.

Sin makes us slaves, and Gomer literally ended up on the auction block, probably because of debts. God told Hosea to buy her back to demonstrate God's faithful love for us. Slaves were typically stripped naked for all to inspect and then sold in the town square. This is the same degradation into which sin seeks to drag us all.

The men gathered to place bids on the stripped body of Hosea's wife, now to become a slave. "Twelve pieces of silver," bid one. "Thirteen," called a voice from the back, a voice she may have dimly remembered. "Fourteen," came the reply. "Fifteen," said Hosea. "Fifteen silver pieces and a bushel of barley." Stepping forward and reaching out to his wife, Hosea spoke, "Fifteen pieces of silver and a bushel and a half of barley." Everyone realized he could not be outbid, and so the other men began to walk away. She was rightly his already, but sin had torn her away. Now he has bought her back with everything he has, and then he drapes her with his love. The conclusion of the story in Hosea 3 says, "So I bought her for fifteen shekels of silver and a homer and a lethech of barley. And I said to her, 'You must dwell as mine for many days. You shall not play the whore, or belong to another man; so will I also be to you'" (Hos. 3:2–3).

If we are in Christ, that is our story as well. Boice comments:

> We were created for intimate fellowship with God and
> for freedom, but we have disgraced ourselves by un-

faithfulness. First we have flirted with and then committed adultery with this sinful world and its values. The world even bid for our soul, offering sex, money, fame, power, and all the other items in which it traffics. But Jesus, our faithful bridegroom and lover, entered the marketplace to buy us back. He bid his own blood. There is no higher bid than that. And we became his. He reclothed us, not in the wretched rags of our old unrighteousness, but in his new robes of righteousness. He has said to us, "You must dwell as mine . . . you shall not belong to another . . . so will I also be to you."[11]

You may have noticed that I have been concluding these chapters with excerpts from Christian hymns. That was not intentional at first, but realizing what I was doing I then recognized how fitting it is considering these great themes of our salvation. How can we not sing, with thoughts of a Savior like this? More importantly, how can we not give all our trust, all our hope, all our love to him, offering to his love the whole of our lives in grateful praise?

I praise the God of grace;
I trust his truth and might;
He calls me his, I call him mine,
My God, my joy, my light.
'Tis he who saveth me,
And freely pardon gives;
I love because he loveth me,
I live because he lives.[12]

8

THE BLOOD
OF CHRIST

Ephesians 1:7

Through his blood.
—Ephesians 1:7

In his majestic study titled *The Cross of Christ,* John
R. W. Stott observes that "every religion and ideol-
ogy has its visual symbol, which illustrates a significant feature
of its history or beliefs." He cites the lotus flower, which sym-
bolizes Buddhism, "because of its wheel shape that is thought
to depict either the cycle of birth and death or the emergence
of beauty and harmony out of the muddy waters of chaos."
Modern Judaism employs the Star of David, which recalls the
Jews' hope for a Messiah out of this their royal line. Islam employs a crescent, an ancient symbol of sovereignty picked up

from Byzantium. Secular ideologies also employ symbols. The Marxist hammer and sickle represents the urban and rural proletariat; the tools are crossed to indicate the unity of industrial laborers with peasant farmers. The sinister, bent cross of the Nazi swastika evoked Germany's pagan past and the ideals of Aryan supremacy.[1]

AN AWKWARD SYMBOL

Christians likewise have their symbols. In the early church's age of persecution, the fish symbol served as a surreptitious way of identifying oneself as a Christian. The Greek word for fish provided an acrostic that had meaning only for church members; the various letters stood for "Jesus Christ, Son of God, Savior." When persecution died down and Christians were able to openly depict their faith, it was the cross that came to the fore. Stott comments on how striking this choice of a symbol was, first of all because of the horror with which the cross was looked upon in the ancient world. He writes, "How could any sane person worship as a god a dead man who had been justly condemned as a criminal and subjected to the most humiliating form of execution? This combination of death, crime and shame put him beyond the pale of respect, let alone of worship."[2]

The Roman orator Cicero condemned crucifixion as "a most cruel and disgusting punishment." "There is no fitting word," he wrote, "that can possibly describe so horrible a deed."[3] The Jews felt the same way, informed by Deuteronomy 21:23 that "anyone who is hung on a tree is under God's curse" (NIV). More recently, Frederick Nietzsche decried the cross as the most abominable decadence, because it offers salvation to the weak, who ought by rights to be destroyed. Other modern thinkers belittle the cross because its related doctrines of God's wrath and human sin and the atonement are, as one put it, "intellectually contemptible and morally outrageous."[4] Ghandi, the great Indian leader, admitted to having once been attracted to Christianity, but what stopped him was the cross. "I could accept Jesus as a martyr," he wrote, "an embodiment of sacrifice, and a divine teacher." But when it came to the saving significance of Christ's death, this was another matter. Ghandi wrote, "That there was anything like a mysterious or miraculous virtue in it, my heart could not accept."[5]

With all that going against it, the cross is hardly an advertiser's dream. If only we could get rid of the cross, some have thought, we could win great masses to Christianity. And yet the cross persists as the emblem of all that Christians hold dear, so that Jesus' followers insist that to remove the cross is to lose everything. What is the greatest scandal to the world, what is most hateful and unacceptable to many about the New Testament depiction of Jesus Christ, is at the same time the most blessed, most cherished, most indispensable and transforming fact of history and theology, to which we cling as that which is most necessary for the salvation of our souls. As Paul put it, "For the word of the cross is folly to those who are perishing, but to us who are being saved it is the power of God." Thus he wrote of himself and all the true church following him, "We preach Christ crucified, a stumbling block to Jews and folly to Gentiles, but to those who are called, both Jews and Greeks, Christ the power of God and the wisdom of God" (1 Cor. 1:18, 23–24).

SACRIFICIAL DEATH

Perhaps what is most noteworthy in Ephesians 1:7 is the offhand manner in which Paul refers to Christ's blood. He writes, "In him we have redemption through his blood, the forgiveness of our trespasses." The lack of explanation here suggests Paul's confidence in his readers' understanding at this point. We know from other letters, such as Romans, that the saving power of Christ's blood was a central feature of Paul's systematic theology. Here in Ephesus, it seems, Paul has freedom simply to mention Christ's blood without elaboration, a happy situation he seldom encountered and one that we should not assume today. It was often necessary for Paul and other apostolic writers—the writer of Hebrews especially comes to mind—to dwell deliberately on the nature and significance of Christ's death, and it is necessary for us to do so today.

It is important for us to know, for instance, that when Paul speaks of Christ's blood it is his death that he specifically has in mind. There are some people who think the reference to blood speaks not of Christ's death but of his life. It is common today to read summaries of the gospel or the doctrine of justification that make no mention of the cross, only the resurrection. Leviticus 17:11 says, "The life . . . is in the blood," and on that basis some interpreters have taught that by pouring out his blood Christ gave access to the power of his life. But the point of that verse is quite the opposite. Since the life is in the blood, blood sacrifice takes the life and causes the sacrifice's death. We have no gospel and no justification except that Christ died for us. Paul makes this connection clear in many places, writing, "He was delivered over to death for our sins" (Rom. 4:25 NIV). "We were reconciled to God," he says, "by the death of his Son" (Rom. 5:10). By taking the cup which in the Lord's Supper signifies Christ's blood, Paul writes, "you proclaim the Lord's death until he comes" (1 Cor. 11:26).

Yet, when we speak of Christ's blood, it is a certain kind of death we have in view. It is essential that Jesus did not die in bed of old age or infirmity; his was a sacrificial death, by which he represented his people before God and vicariously suffered in our place.

All this was prefigured in the Old Testament sacrifices.

100

There were different kinds of sacrifices under the old covenant, but at the heart of them all were the sin and guilt offerings. The Book of Leviticus presents these with several common features. First, the animal to be sacrificed had to be without blemish or flaw. God's people were not permitted to offer the weakest and least desirable from their flocks, but only the best and strongest and most pure. This pointed forward to the sinlessness of Christ; himself unblemished by sin, he alone was able to offer himself for others.

Second, God graciously provided the animal as a substitute to bear the penalty the sinner deserved. The key theological terms here are *vicarious* and *substitutionary*. The substitute suffered vicariously, that is, on behalf of the sinner.

Third, the blood of this sacrifice was sprinkled on the altar before the Lord, so that, having seen the sure evidence of the sacrificial death, God would forgive the sinner who came by faith in his gracious provision. In many cases, the blood was likewise sprinkled on the one who had sinned, to show the removal of guilt. This whole procedure was called the making of atonement; over and over Moses summarizes in Leviticus, "the priest shall make atonement for them, and they shall be forgiven" (Lev. 4:20, 26, 31, 35; 5:13, 18; 6:7; 12:8; 14:31).

The Book of Hebrews most explicitly makes the connection between these Old Testament sacrifices and the death of Jesus Christ. Like those earlier types, Jesus' death was a vicarious, substitutionary atonement. He suffered the death others deserved, in their place and on their behalf, to make atonement for their sins. Hebrews 9:13–14 notes that the old animal sacrifices were able to cleanse people outwardly and ceremonially. "How much more," asks the writer, "will the blood of Christ, who through the eternal Spirit offered himself without blemish to God, purify our conscience from dead works to serve the living God." Unlike the blood of bulls and goats, Christ's blood is an effectual, spiritual sacrifice. Therefore, Jesus cried in his death, "It is finished" (John 19:30). Hebrews 9:26–28 argues that no other sacrifice than Christ's is needed: "He has appeared once for all at the end of the ages to put away sin by the sacrifice of himself. And just as it is appointed for man to die once, and after that comes judgment, so Christ [was] offered once to bear the sins of many."

All this was made vivid in the final week of Jesus' life, which coincided with the feast of Passover. While our Lord entered Jerusalem for what we call Palm Sunday, the sacrificial lambs were being herded by the thousands into the city. This was God's way of saying, "Here is your true sacrifice, what the lambs had all along merely symbolized!" Later, when Jesus was crucified, the hammer strokes nailed his hands and feet to the cross at the precise moment the Jews were slaying their Passover lambs. This is what John the Baptist, the final prophet of the old dispensation, was getting at when he spoke of Jesus: "Behold, the Lamb of God, who takes away the sin of the world!" (John 1:29).

All of this is bound up in Paul's mention of the blood of Christ—Jesus' vicarious, substitutionary, atoning death as the true and only instrument by which a sinner may be forgiven and reconciled to God.

The Terminology of Atonement

Every club, profession, or political body has its specialized terminology, and Christianity is no different. People complain when a preacher uses technical theological terms, but in a time when people remember multiple ten-digit passwords and enough technical knowledge about their computers to fill a textbook, I am unashamed to do so when it comes to the most important fact of history, the death of Christ. Technical terms aid us by affording precision in our thinking, and that is no less the case when it comes to the significance of the blood of Christ.

The Bible presents Christ's death from a number of perspectives, such as the temple setting, the law court, the marketplace, and the personal relationship. In each case, the core idea is that of vicarious substitution, and from each point of view Christ is presented as the mediator between God and man who solves the problem of our sin. Having examined the marketplace in the previous chapter, let's consider Christ's death from the other three vantage points.

The perspective of the temple setting. The word *atonement* speaks of a sacrifice dealing with sin, and the Bible describes this in terms of two effects. The first of these, *propitiation,* is directed toward God, to the problem of God's just wrath against sin. The Bible assures us that God is angry not merely at sin but at sinners, as the example of Sodom and Gomorrah so vividly demonstrates. But God's wrath is different from the impetuous, often sinful anger of human beings. God's wrath is righteous. It is good and holy and appropriate. As J. I. Packer notes, God's wrath "is never the capricious, self-indulgent, irritable, morally ignoble thing that human anger so often is. It is, instead, a right and necessary reaction to objective moral evil."[6] This being the case, we as sinners need to be saved from God. God is rightly angry with us, and to propitiate this wrath Christ died for us. God poured out the infinite hell of his wrath upon his Son—who by the power of his infinite life could bear it—and thus God's wrath is turned aside from us, or propitiated, by the blood of Christ.

Here, from this perspective, is the gospel, that God made provision for the propitiation of his wrath, through the blood of his Son. Paul says in Romans 3:24–25 that we "are justified by his grace as a gift, through the redemption that is in Christ Jesus, whom God put forward as a propitiation by his blood, to be received by faith." Therefore, according to this teaching, Christians are saved from God. That is our great need, to escape his holy wrath. And we are saved by God, who sent his Son to propitiate God's righteous anger through the blood of his cross.

Christ's death has the Godward effect of propitiation, symbolized by sprinkling of blood before him on the altar. But it also has an effect on us, symbolized by the sprinkling of blood upon the sinner. This is called *expiation,* that is, the removal of our sin. The apostle John wrote of this: "If we confess our sins, he is faithful and just to forgive us our sins and to cleanse us from all unrighteousness" (1 John 1:9). That is expiation—the cleansing of our sin.

Christ's blood does more than turn God's wrath from us; it makes us clean. How significant this is for sinners, who though forgiven feel dirty before God and man. But if Christ has died for you, he has cleansed you with his blood! Your sin is taken away. One of the rites on the Old Testament Day of Atonement symbolized this. Leviticus 16:10 tells us that the high priest laid his hands on a goat, transferring the people's sins onto this substitute. The scapegoat, as it was called, was then led into the wilderness, never to be seen again, just as our sins are taken away by the blood of Christ. The writer of Hebrews emphasized the importance of this for our personal communion with God. Christ, he notes, has opened the way to God by his blood and now serves before God as our interceding priest. "Therefore," he says, "let us draw near [to God] with a true heart in full assurance of faith, with our hearts sprinkled clean from an evil conscience" (Heb. 10:19–22). That is something to sing about, and it is not morbid when Christians therefore rejoice:

> *There is a fountain filled with blood,*
> *Drawn from Emmanuel's veins.*
> *And sinners plunged beneath that flood*
> *Lose all their guilty stains.*[7]

The perspective of the law court. Christ's death is presented from the perspective of the temple, in propitiation and expiation, but also from that of the law court. This is most explicit in Romans 3, where Paul first goes out of his way to show that "all have sinned" by breaking God's law. There is an accusation and a trial to take place, and Paul assures us that since all have sinned, "by works of the law no human being will be justified in [God's] sight" (Rom. 3:20). Our problem again is God, now expressed in terms of his unyielding law. In the next verse Paul declares the good news of Christianity, that "now a righteousness from God . . . has been made known" (Rom. 3:21 NIV). While we have no righteousness to present in God's court but rather are bound to be convicted and condemned as lawbreakers, God has a righteousness to give us so that we might be justified through faith in Christ.

Here, the key term is *justification,* which means to be found just in God's court. Along with it is the phrase *imputed righteousness,* which is how we are justified. Though we are unrighteous, we are declared righteous, not by our merits but by the righteousness of Christ, which is imputed or credited to us. Paul explains, "The righteousness of God [comes] through faith in Jesus Christ for all who believe. For there is no distinction: for all have sinned and fall short of the glory of God, and are justified by his grace as a gift, through the redemption that is in Christ Jesus, whom God put forward as a propitiation by his blood, to be received by faith" (Rom. 3:22–25). Legally, Christ's blood provides justification in God's court to all who trust in him, so that as Paul went on to write, "There is therefore now no condemnation for those who are in Christ Jesus" (Rom. 8:1). This, too, is something to sing about:

Jesus, thy blood and righteousness,
My beauty are, my glorious dress;

'Midst flaming worlds, in these arrayed,
With joy shall I lift up my head.

Bold shall I stand in thy great day;
For who aught to my charge shall lay?
Fully absolved through these I am
From sin and fear, from guilt and shame.[8]

The perspective of the personal relationship. We have considered the temple setting and the law court. However, the biblical language of Christ's blood also speaks of a relationship that has been sundered but is repaired by the precious blood of Christ. The problem of sin is twofold. God is alienated from us, unwilling and unable in his holiness to fellowship with soiled sinners. We in turn are alienated from God, bound as we are in the slavery of our sinful condition. Christ died to bridge this gulf. His blood causes God to forgive our sins, since the debt has been paid, the offense atoned for, his righteous wrath averted. Likewise, Christ redeems us from our bondage in sin so that through his cross we are bought back from sin and brought back to God. The result is *reconciliation,* which Paul extols in one of the great statements in the New Testament:

> All this is from God, who through Christ reconciled us
> to himself and gave us the ministry of reconciliation;
> that is, in Christ God was reconciling the world to himself, not counting their trespasses against them. . . . We
> implore you on behalf of Christ, be reconciled to God.
> For our sake he made him to be sin who knew no sin,
> so that in him we might become the righteousness of
> God. (2 Cor. 5:18–21)

Atonement, propitiation, expiation, justification, imputed righteousness, forgiveness, redemption, reconciliation—what a great gospel is contained in all these terms, and all through the shed blood of Jesus Christ! Putting it all together, we are saved from God—his wrath no longer turned against us, his curse no longer on us; we are saved by God, who sent his only Son to die in our place and for our salvation; and we are saved to God, who now calls sinners to repent and believe, so that all who will come may be fully restored to his love.[9] The wonder of this grace through the blood of God's Son never ceases to fill us with joyful praise, and again it is in song that our hearts reply:

> *And can it be that I should gain*
> *An interest in the Saviour's blood?*
> . . . .
> *Amazing love! How can it be,*
> *that thou, my God, shouldst die for me?*[10]

BLOODY RELIGION

With all that said, Christians have to confess the truth of our critics' complaint, that ours is a "bloody religion." One such critic is the Episcopal bishop John Shelby Spong, who wrote a book titled *Why Christianity Must Change or Die*. At the heart of his objection to historic Christianity is this matter of Christ's shed blood. According to Spong, such bizarre and primitive religious views can only repulse the modern man and woman. "I would choose to loathe," he writes, "rather than to worship a deity who required the sacrifice of his son."[11] Spong, and others like him, think it is time the Christian church dispenses with the ugly symbol of the cross, which he calls "an image that has to go."[12] Yet, to his dismay, Christians still "cling to the old rugged cross";[13] they sing still, "O precious is the flow that makes me white as snow; no other fount I know, nothing but the blood of Jesus."[14]

107

One thing is revealed in all of this: your view of everything is determined by your attitude toward the blood of Christ. P. T. Forsyth was right when he wrote, "Christ is to us just what his cross is."[15] If the cross is an offense, then a crucified Christ is also an offense. He must be gotten rid of, replaced with some other religious icon. If the cross is foolishness, as it was to the Greeks of Paul's day, then Christ must be shunned lest you be embarrassed in proper society. If the cross is a stumbling block, as it was to the Jews, then Christ must be destroyed and his followers persecuted. But if you look to the cross as a guilty sinner and see there your only hope of salvation, then Christ is to you a Savior and you will cling with all of your might to his cross.

There is a reason the world hates the blood of Christ, for the cross condemns the world. It is, as D. Martyn Lloyd-Jones says,

> a standing condemnation of every view and philosophy which says that men and women by their own efforts can reconcile themselves to God, or that they can atone for their sin. To all such views, the answer of the cross is that no one can do this. The cross is the proclamation of the insufficiency of mankind, and people dislike it because of that, for they believe in themselves and in their own power.[16]

The blood of Christ insults the self-reliance of this world, and it does so by proclaiming all the biblical doctrines of salvation. The cross reveals God's wrath against our sin. We like to think that sin amounts to little, that God is not perturbed, that forgiveness is automatic, and that God is sure to accept us. But Christ's blood says that even when his precious Son bore the guilt of our sin, God poured out on him the fullness of his wrath. "Father, Father, why have you forsaken me?" cried the sin-bearing Christ, and equally forsaken is everyone not covered through faith in his blood. People are likewise offended by the gospel's offer of salvation. God's grace declares that we are failures, we are guilty, we are damned. God has to come and save us; God's Son had to come "to seek and to save the lost" (Luke 19:10). In all these ways the cross offends by declaring us sinners, saved only by the grace of God in Christ.

But what if we look to the cross and admit that we are not righteous, if we realize that God rightly punishes every sin? What if we admit that we are helpless to save ourselves, hopeless save for God's grace? If you can say that, if you gaze on the blood of Christ and cry for him to be your Savior, then what is contemptible to the world is precious in your sight. For Christ's blood tells us that a Savior has come. Christ has taken our sins onto himself. He has shed his blood in our place. He has propitiated God's wrath and expiated our sins; he has won forgiveness of our sins so that we might be found just before God; he has redeemed us from the power and guilt of sin; he has reconciled God to us and us to God, all through faith in his blood.

To all who believe, the cross of Christ, the blood of Christ, reveals something exceedingly precious, even the love of God for sinners. It says, "God so loved the world that he gave his only Son, that whoever believes in him should not perish but have eternal life" (John 3:16). It teaches, "God shows his love for us in that while we were still sinners, Christ died for us" (Rom. 5:8).

You see, then, why Christians rejoice in the blood of Christ, why we claim no higher allegiance, no greater glory, no brighter hope, than that which is symbolized with the crossed wooden beams, which tell the world, "His banner over me was love" (Song 2:4). If you understand that, if you come to God through the shed blood of Christ, then you will lift your praise to God, along with the apostle, who writes here, "Blessed

109

be the God and Father of our Lord Jesus Christ, who has blessed us in Christ with every spiritual blessing in the heavenly places . . . . In [Christ] we have redemption through his blood, the forgiveness of our trespasses, according to the riches of [God's] grace" (Eph. 1:3, 7). "Far be it from me to boast except in the cross of our Lord Jesus Christ," Paul elsewhere wrote (Gal. 6:14). And to Christ be all the glory, all the praise, and all the love in our hearts. Amen.

9

THE SALVATION
MYSTERY

Ephesians 1:9–10

> *Making known to us the mystery of his will,*
> *according to his purpose, which he set forth in Christ*
> *as a plan for the fullness of time, to unite all things*
> *in him, things in heaven and things on earth.*
> —Ephesians 1:9–10

There are two story lines written into the fabric of this world. The first and most familiar is the tragedy, which is the story of our world apart from God's saving intervention. This is the story of the fall, with its themes of failure, alienation, and curse. It is the story the Bible tells just after its beginning. The story of the fall in Genesis 3 follows hard on the story of creation in Genesis 1 and Genesis 2. Adam and Eve dis-

111

obeyed God's command by eating of the tree of the knowledge of good and evil. They fell under God's curse and were cast out from the garden. As sin worked in the generations that followed, this story of tragedy continued, with Cain's murder of Abel in Genesis 4 and the growth of his wicked line in Genesis 5, on to the dispersing of all the nations in God's judgment at the Tower of Babel in Genesis 11. This is the story of tragedy that is written into our sinful world, and its pattern is always the same: sin against God, followed by alienation from God, failure, and misery.

TWO STORIES: TRAGEDY AND SALVATION

Literary scholars tell us that certain requirements must be met for a story to qualify as a true tragedy. First, there must be initial greatness and goodness, with hope for glory and blessing. The tragic hero is always a person of virtue and lofty potential who is overcome by a fatal flaw. This is how the Bible presents humankind. Created by God with goodness and the stamp of his glorious image, humanity nonetheless fell into sin. Sin is the fatal flaw of our race, and it always proves to be our undoing. This is the story told by the pen of human history on a broad scale. Empires rise and thrive in glory only to decay, to tragically fall and disappear into oblivion. Tragedy is also told on a smaller scale through our individual experiences. Our capacity for achievement is undermined by our sin. Marriages begin so brightly but are soon dimmed by sin. Careers launch with great expectations but soon lead to struggle and often to disappointments that embitter the soul. God's curse to the first sinner, Adam, still dominates our tragic reality in this world:

> By the sweat of your face
>   you shall eat bread,
> till you return to the ground,
>   . . . .

112

for you are dust,
    and to dust you shall return. (Gen. 3:19)

William Shakespeare was the master of tragedy, and one of his most famous tragic plays is *Macbeth*. This is the story of a Scottish nobleman, renowned for valor and faithfulness, who came under temptation's power and fell prey to sin. His moral failure and guilt-wracked conscience ultimately led him to ruin. This is the tragic story, told in epic terms, that is familiar to us all in our ordinary lives. This is why stories like this are so irresistible in movies and in books; like it or not, it is our story, and we connect with it because of the similar tragedy of our own experience. Shakespeare's great character Macbeth speaks in a way we all have felt when he gives his classic description of life as a grand tragedy:

> *Life's but a walking shadow, a poor player*
> *That struts and frets his hour upon the stage*
> *And then is heard no more. It is a tale*
> *Told by an idiot, full of sound and fury*
> *Signifying nothing.*

I said that there are two story lines in this world. The first is tragedy, and the second is salvation. Whereas tragedy is the storyof failure, alienation, and curse, salvation tells of triumph, redemption, and blessing. Here is the voice of laughter heard beside the sobbing tears. We find this story line in Shakespeare's comedies, which so often end in wedding scenes, all the characters rejoined in hope and joy. We also find it in fairy tales, which tell us that in the end, "they lived happily ever after." We may think of fairy tales and fantasies as unreal, unbelievable, but isn't it interesting that we still read them to our children generation after generation? Surely they connect with our secret and deep hopes that there is something to it for us, there is a way to the happy ending we long for.

These are the two stories of this world. There is tragedy, which we know from lived experience, from the microscope and telescope of historical observation. Then there is salvation, the story that does not arise from our experience but breaks in from outside, the way that dawn's first light breaks upon the darkness of the night. The salvation story comes from God and relies upon the revelation in his Word. This is what Christianity presents to a world that though fallen and cursed cannot forget its hope of glory and blessing—what Paul calls the mystery of salvation revealed by God to this world, the claim that salvation will overthrow the fall, that redemption will conquer alienation, that God's blessing will undo the curse of sin. This is the mystery to which the prophets pointed:

> The wolf shall dwell with the lamb,
>   and the leopard shall lie down with the young
>   goat,
> and the calf and the lion and the fattened calf to-
>   gether;
>   and a little child shall lead them. (Isa. 11:6)

It is this salvation story that Paul refers to in our passage as "the mystery of [God's] will" as it is manifested and made real through the appearing of our Lord Jesus Christ.

REVELATION AND REDEMPTIVE HISTORY

When I speak of these two stories, it is not fiction that I have in mind, although here is an example where art follows reality. These are not merely two stories but two histories working side by side in this world. There is the history taught in secular textbooks, which starts with the record of prehistoric civilization and progresses through the Mesopotamian empires to Greece and then Rome, the Dark Ages followed by the rise of Europe, the rise of New World nations like America, and now the new global age. The most penetrating modern and postmodern thinkers look on this history and label it hopeless, meaningless, and cursed. For all the excitement, they categorize it under the heading of tragedy, rendering on it Macbeth's verdict: all sound and fury, signifying nothing.

But, says our passage, there is another history, God's redemptive history, which is all the while working forward according to a very different story line, that of salvation. This is what Paul has been tracing in this great doxology in Ephesians 1. This history begins before records were kept and empires began leaving their traces, indeed, before creation itself. This history began in the mind of God, entering into time through his great redemptive work, which centers on our Lord Jesus Christ. It is a history that has a predetermined, prerecorded finale, namely, the glorification and blessing of God's redeemed people in and through the exaltation of his Son. This redemptive history reflects God's plan of the ages, omnipotently and mysteriously pressing on toward the goal stated in Ephesians 1:10, "To unite all things in [Christ], things in heaven and things on earth."

The relationship between the history and the story, between God's redemptive work, by which he does what is needed for our salvation, and God's revelatory Word, by which he confirms and explains it to us, is important to Paul. The previous couple of verses spoke of God lavishing his grace on believers through the saving work of Jesus Christ. Now in Ephesians 1:9 he speaks of God revealing this to us, "making known to us the mystery of his will, according to his purpose."

Paul explains this relationship between God's works and his Word in one of his great summary statements, 1 Corinthians 15:3–4: "For I delivered to you as of first importance what I also received: that Christ died for our sins in accordance with the Scriptures, that he was buried, that he was raised on the third day in accordance with the Scriptures." This reminds us that God's saving works are not just random acts of kindness but flow from a divine plan that has been revealed to the world through his divinely authorized messengers. It is of the greatest significance that Jesus' first coming—his life and death and resurrection—was in fulfillment of the Scriptures, and this is a great proof of the divine source of these events. God not only has done what we need, but also has revealed to us his salvation, so that we may enter into it through faith.

Here we encounter for the first time a word that occurs throughout the Book of Ephesians, *mystery*. When Paul speaks of God's revelation as a mystery he means something different from what we tend to mean by using this word. He does not mean that we are given clues with the task of figuring out their secret, the way a mystery novel challenges us to figure out if the butler or the cook committed the murder. For Paul, the mystery of God's will is a reality that can be known only by revelation and can be fully known only as God's redemptive and revelatory history ripens to maturity. The mystery of salvation is something no one could ever figure out by reason alone, not because it is irrational but because it is not revealed by the common experience of life, much less by the conventional wisdom of this world. Paul uses *mystery* seven times in Ephesians, speaking of "the mystery of [God's] will," "the mystery of the gospel," and "the mystery of Christ." The mystery is the salvation story made known by God's revelation through the prophets and apostles and brought to full expression in God's timing through the person and work of Jesus Christ.

If we think about this we will realize what exciting news this is. Paul is saying that God's will—which men and women can never know through their efforts—is revealed in the gospel. This is the most stupendous news ever, that the mind

116

of God is made known to humanity. God's very plan for history is revealed here. This is what Christianity deals with and brings to the world—not a therapeutic program for earthly happiness, not a political-action agenda, not a power game by one racial or ethnic or religious group against others. Christianity presents revelation from God regarding his otherwise secret plan for saving the fallen world. It is the mystery of God's will made known by his revealed Word.

In these verses, Paul emphasizes themes we have already encountered. First, God's is a sovereign will—it is "the mystery of his will, according to his purpose" (Eph. 1:9). God is not consulting us, nor is our message the product of human investigation or consideration. It is revelation, a disclosing of God's sovereign, almighty will. Furthermore, we are reminded here that God's purpose is and always has been focused on his Son, Jesus Christ. We worship God through Jesus Christ not merely because Jesus helps us or because we can relate to him but because God's eternal purpose is centered on him and manifested through him.

Paul adds, in Ephesians 1:10 that this is "a plan for the fullness of time," or, as the New International Version puts it, it all is "put into effect when the times will have reached their fulfillment." This tells us there is a progressive nature to God's redemptive work and to his revelation of it. God placed Adam and Eve in the garden and gave the covenant of works by which humankind might be justified. Adam failed, and we fell under the curse of sin. But God had prepared the intervention of his Son through the covenant of grace, so that all salvation would be through and in Christ. God was not caught off guard by the fall; immediately he made great promises of an offspring who would suffer but would conquer for our salvation (Gen. 3:15).

God pressed forward with his redemptive plan through long generations. He called Abraham to go to Canaan and begin the series of events that created Israel as a nation and brought them into the Promised Land. God gave the law to Moses to preserve the nation and teach the people to look for a Savior. Over long centuries, Israel lived before God, their religious institutions informing the world of his salvation, their existence proving that God had not abandoned the fallen and sinful human race. But even the Jews fell into sin, breaking the covenant God gave through Moses. Yet God remained faithful, and even this served to point forward to a new covenant in a Savior who would fulfill all that Israel had failed to do under God's law.

Meanwhile, events outside of Israel were conspiring to prepare the way not merely for the coming of the Messiah but for the spread of his gospel throughout the world. Greek philosophy flowered, providing so many of the thought categories the gospel would later employ, as well as a common language for the ancient world with which to learn of it. Roman power arose, providing peace so that people and commerce and thoughts could travel freely from region to region. In all these ways, God—not consulting our wisdom and not seeking our approval—prepared the world for his Son, that he might accomplish the works needed for our salvation and that we might hear it and believe. At just the right time, Jesus came and died for our sins, he rose from the dead, and he sent forth his apostles to make known this mystery of God's will, a salvation plan that continues even now through the gospel until its culmination in the gathering of all things under Christ.

TOGETHER UNDER ONE HEAD

This is what Paul wants us to know. For by believing in Christ we enter into the knowledge and the blessing of God's saving purpose in Christ. Paul wants us to know not only our present reality and the past that has led up to it. In Ephesians

1:10 he takes us into the future. The mystery of God's will is a salvation story that is not yet finished, and Paul wants us to know the end. It is a history that has not yet reached its goal, namely, "to unite all things in [Christ], things in heaven and things on earth."

The key expression is "to unite all things," or as the NIV puts it, "to bring . . . together under one head," which in the Greek is a single word, *anakephaaioō*. In Romans 13:9 Paul uses the same word to speak of the summing up of all the commandments under the heading of love. Here, his point is that history has a destination, a purpose, and a climax, and that these are all contained in the gathering of all things together under the lordship of Jesus Christ.

This runs against the grain of modern thought, which assures us that history has no purpose and no goal. It has become fashionable for skeptics to speak in the manner of one liberal scholar, G. N. Clark, who asserts, "There is no secret and no plan in history to be discovered. I do not believe that any future consummation could make sense of all the irrationalities of preceding ages." Andre Maurois said, "Why are we here on this puny mud-heap spinning in infinite space? I have not the slightest idea, and I am quite convinced that no one has the least idea."[1] That kind of thinking is given as a justification for godless living; why should we live by any higher code if life is all meaningless? As Paul once wrote, "If the dead are not raised, 'Let us eat and drink, for tomorrow we die' " (1 Cor. 15:32).

We ought to look with sympathy on such unbelieving people. The meaning of history is a dark mystery to them, partly because the only history they know—the tragic story of a sinful world—is in fact hopeless, and if we did not have the revelation of God we would no doubt think that same way. But theirs is also a culpable ignorance; their minds are willingly shut to the Word of God and its story of salvation. God's Word says there is a purpose to history and therefore to our lives. God has revealed that purpose, namely, that he is uniting all things in Christ, things in heaven and on earth.

Paul has been praising God for salvation, extolling Jesus as the means of our redemption, which is "through his blood" (Eph. 1:7). But now he shows Jesus as the end of our salvation, so that we and the entire cosmos are redeemed under and into the headship of Jesus Christ, whom God has exalted in the highest. P. T. O'Brien explains, "Christ is the one *in whom* God chooses to sum up the cosmos, the one in whom he restores harmony to the universe. He is the focal point, not simply the means, the instrument . . . through whom all this occurs."[2]

Remarkably, Paul says that "all things" will be brought together under Christ, things "in heaven and . . . on earth." He does not mean by this a universal salvation in which none are condemned, for that would involve a fatal inconsistency in his thought and in the Bible. It is a universality within redemption, a bringing together all that has been saved and restored by and in and unto the Lord Jesus Christ.

There are two ways we can properly understand this. Charles Hodge understands this "all things" as including only those believers now in heaven and those still on earth, since the context is one of salvation through Christ's blood, and these are the objects of his death. It is the whole company of the redeemed that is brought together under Christ, along with the holy angels who serve God and minister to them. Hodge says, "The apostle refers to the union of all the people of God . . . in one body under Jesus Christ their head. They are to be constituted an everlasting kingdom."[3]

Andrew Lincoln points out, however, that "heaven and earth" was a common Jewish expression for the whole of created reality. Paul teaches elsewhere that the whole creation came under the effects of sin and looks forward to final deliverance through Christ. Romans 8:19–21 says, "The creation waits with eager longing for the revealing of the sons of God. . . . the creation itself will be set free from its bondage to decay and obtain the freedom of the glory of the children of God." This, then, is the "all things" of which Paul writes in our passage, that at the end of history the entire created order, subjected to corruption in the fall, will be restored to unity, harmony, order, and eternal glory under the lordship of Jesus Christ.

It is significant that this Greek word *anakephalaioō* contains the prefix *ana,* which means "again." This is a restoration, bringing things together again under Christ, and as such it presupposes a prior disintegration, an alienation and separation that is the result of sin. There once was a perfect condition. It was lost, but now it will be restored through and in Christ. You see how important the first chapters of Genesis are to the Christian worldview. There was a tragedy, but now there is a salvation. There was alienation, but now there is redemption; there was separation, but now there is reconciliation; there is a curse, but blessing lies ahead. Therefore, if realism toward this world demands that we embrace tragedy and its story—and such realism does require this—there is a higher realism that Christians embrace, a realism toward God and his saving intervention. There is a real fall, but also a restoration that is more real still. This is now our story, and we look forward to the bringing of all things together again under Jesus Christ.

The story of the fall in the Book of Genesis comes to completion in the tragic tale of the Tower of Babel (Gen. 11). I have said that the story of sin involves separation and alienation, and Genesis 11 provides a classic instance. The peoples had gathered in rebellion against God, joining to build the great tower for their own glory. God was angered, and he brought confusion to their languages so they could not understand one another. As a result they were unable to work in harmony and were scattered through the world. It is fascinating to realize, then, that the age of Christ began with the day of Pentecost, which is the redemptive counterpart to that tragic tale. Where the fall ends, the story of redemption begins and starts working back, undoing the work of sin. In this same way, Pentecost saw the undoing of what happened at the Tower of Babel. People from all the different languages resulting from that long-distant judgment were enabled by the Spirit to understand one another, and they became one again. The separation caused by sin was overthrown by the reunion brought about in Christ. Jesus Christ, having ascended to heaven in power, poured out his Spirit to effect reconciliation in himself. That is just one example, a foretaste, of a whole cosmic reconciliation that will come sweeping into creation when Christ returns with glory in his second coming. Christ's saving work picks up where the story of sin ends; he redeems what is fallen, he restores what has been lost, he brings together what has been alienated and scattered in sin.

Revelation 11:15 shows us how complete this will be in the end. There, the voices in heaven are heard celebrating the completion of what Paul writes of here in advance: "The kingdom of the world has become the kingdom of our Lord and of his Christ, and he shall reign for ever and ever." The prophet Isaiah foresaw this glorified world, rejoicing, "They shall not hurt or destroy in all my holy mountain; for the earth shall be full of the knowledge of the LORD as the waters cover the sea" (Isa. 11:9). Redemption in Christ involves a whole restoration of the fallen creation, a total undoing of all the work of sin and an advancement of creation into the harmonious glory originally intended by God. Therefore, our task in this present age is to participate in that work with him, serving as agents of righteousness and peace and harmony, especially as heralds of this gospel of salvation that proclaims peace on earth. "Your kingdom come, your will be done," we pray, and that is our desire, the extension of God's saving reign for which we labor even now.

LIVING BACK FROM THE END

Most stories are ruined by knowing the end in advance, but not this one. That is because, even with this revealing of the great salvation mystery, our minds can scarcely conceive of what it will be like when all is restored in the glory of Christ's ultimate reign. God may safely tell us the ending without spoiling any of the excitement.

I want to conclude with a scene from John Bunyan's *Pilgrim's Progress* that shows how the story of every believer ends. Christian, the hero of the story, and his companion named Hopeful had been journeying toward the Celestial City and had passed through many trials and dangers, just as we must do in this life. Finally, he passed through the waters of death, and Bunyan depicts what happened as Christian approached God's city and was united with Christ in glory.

Now, upon the bank of the river, on the other side, they saw the two Shining Men again, who there waited for them. . . . The city stood upon a mighty hill; but the pilgrims went up that hill with ease, because they had these two men to lead them up by the arms: also they had left their mortal garments behind them in the river. . . . They went up here with much agility and speed, though the foundation upon which the city was framed was higher than the clouds. . . .

The talk they had with the Shining Ones was about the glory of the place, who told them that the beauty and glory of it was inexpressible. There, said they, is the Mount Zion, the heavenly Jerusalem, the innumerable company of angels, and the spirits of just men made perfect. You are going now, said they, to the paradise of God, wherein you shall see the tree of life, and eat of the never-fading fruits thereof; and when you come there, you shall have white robes given you, and your walk and talk shall be every day with the King, even all the days of eternity. . . .

The men then asked, What must we do in the holy place? To whom it was answered, You must there receive the comfort of all your toil, and have joy for all your sorrow; you must reap what you have sown, even the fruit of all your prayers and tears, and sufferings for the King by the way. In that place you must wear crowns of gold, and enjoy the perpetual sight and visions of the Holy One; for there "you shall see him as he is."

Bunyan's vision concludes:

These two men went in at the gate; and lo, as they entered, they were transfigured, and they had raiment put on that shone like gold. . . . All the bells in the city rang again for joy, and it was said unto them, "Enter ye into the joy of your Lord." I looked in after them; and behold, the city shone like the sun; the streets also were paved with gold, and in them walked many men, with crowns on their heads, palms in their hands, and golden harps to sing praises withal. . . . And after that they shut up the gates; which, when I had seen, I wished myself among them.[4]

Understand that this is not just great literature, but a true salvation story. It is our future, our destiny, if we are in Christ, according to the glorious plan of God, the mystery of his will revealed in his Word. I don't know about you, but this changes

124

my life, changes the way I want to live today, and gives me hope and joy unspeakable and a desire to live now for that day to come. And I want to tell others this secret to eternal life, the mystery that is now made known, the forgiveness of sins through faith in Jesus Christ. This is what gives purpose and meaning to my life: to please and serve and glorify our wonderful God, who has planned all this in Christ, according to his own good pleasure, and to the praise of his glorious grace. I pray that it will do the same for you.

10

THE GLORIOUS PLAN OF GOD

Ephesians 1:11–13

*In him we have obtained an inheritance, having been
predestined according to the purpose of him who works all
things according to the counsel of his will, so that we who were
the first to hope in Christ might be to the praise of his glory.
In him you also, when you heard the word of truth,
the gospel of your salvation, and believed in him,
were sealed with the promised Holy Spirit.*
—Ephesians 1:11–13

One of the Bible's most striking descriptions of God is
that of the potter at the potter's wheel. We find it in
Jeremiah 18, where the prophet was told, "Go down to the potter's house, and there I will let you hear my words" (Jer. 18:2).

Jeremiah found the potter shaping the clay on the potter's wheel, "working it," we are told, "as seemed best to him" (Jer. 18:4). God explained, "O house of Israel, can I not do with you as this potter has done? . . . Like the clay in the potter's hand, so are you in my hand" (Jer. 18:6).

There are three parts to this illustration. First there is the potter, a figure that speaks of God's sovereign authority over men and women and nations, but also his interest and involvement with what he is making. G. Campbell Morgan observes, "Looking at the potter as he sits at the wheel and places his hand upon the clay . . . I see his keen interest as the clay changes its form under his fingers. . . . I see his close and unvarying attention to his work; his eye is never lifted from the clay while the wheel revolves and his hand is molding. . . . I also recognize his power . . . infinite so far as the clay is concerned."[1]

Second is the clay, which is molded according to the potter's will and is suitable for his purpose. Thus is humanity in its spiritual nature, our capacity to reflect God's artistry and purpose. Third is the potter's wheel, which speaks of circumstances God employs as tools to mold his people, who are his workmanship. Isaiah therefore says, "We are the clay, and you are the potter; we are all the work of your hand" (Isa. 64:8).

GOD'S SOVEREIGN PLAN

This image fits Paul's way of thinking in Ephesians nicely. One of his chief themes here is the sovereignty of God, and in Ephesians 1:11 he returns to it. He writes, "In him we have . . . been predestined according to the purpose of him who works all things according to the counsel of his will, so that we who were the first to hope in Christ might be to the praise of his glory" (Eph. 1:11–12). God has a plan in which he is utterly sovereign, according to which the salvation of Christians was predestined, all to the glory of his name. Here we have the potter, the vessels he is shaping, and also a plan by which he works all things so that his artistry is revealed in glorious display.

This is one of the great comforting truths of Scripture, that God is working according to a sovereign plan and that everything happens according to his will. We think of what this meant to the Jewish exiles in the time of Jeremiah. Jerusalem was under siege, and a great many Jews had already been carted off into exile. How distressing it was to see their whole way of life destroyed, foreign idols exalted, and pagan lords holding sway over the people of the true and living God. God comforted his people with a message of his sovereignty: "For I know the plans I have for you, declares the LORD, plans for wholeness and not for evil, to give you a future and a hope. Then you will call upon me and come and pray to me, and I will hear you" (Jer. 29:11–12).

Christians rightly apply this to their lives: God has a plan for his people that is working for their good. Thus we are assured that no trial we experience is outside of his control, that through faith we will arrive in a blessed place that God has planned and to which he is leading us, so that our trials, however great, are but the turns of the wheel as God fashions our character for his glory.

It is this kind of sovereignty that Paul sets before us in Ephesians 1:11. Looking at the terms he uses and the ideas he sets forth, we see the extent of sovereignty he has in mind. He says we have been predestined; that is, our lives were foreordained, our salvation especially was determined in advance by God. Some people try to water down the idea of predestination by saying that it is according to God's foreknowledge of our believing. That throws our assurance back onto our resources, so that God's choosing of us relies on our choosing God, with the result that at least some of the glory for salvation goes to us. This verse, perhaps more than any other in Scripture, refutes that teaching. Paul says we have been predestined. But according to what principle does God predestine those who are saved? Paul could not answer the question more emphatically, in a way that radically shuts out any ultimate reliance on human will or effort or activity. We are predestined, he says, according to God's plan.

That leads to another key term, namely, God's purpose. God's plan works out everything according to his purpose. Salvation is directed to a goal that is God's idea, his sovereign choice. It is his will, not ours, that determines everything. Furthermore, God's plan has oversight; God "works all things." God works his plan—he who originated it and planned it also oversees its execution. He is working in history and in our circumstances "according to the counsel of his will." Finally, it all has an object and end, namely, "the praise of his glory." You will not find a more complete statement of God's sovereignty in salvation, or one as foolproof against denial. This statement of God's sovereignty follows the exact progression that Paul employs in the great doxology of Romans 11:36. That verse says, "For from him and through him and to him are all things." So it is in our salvation. It is "from him," that is, it originates from his purpose and will, and "through him" as he works it all out, and it is "to him," that is, to the praise of his glory. Therefore, as Paul concludes that doxology, "To him be glory forever. Amen."

All through these studies I have been asking, "What is a Christian?" Here we have yet another answer. According to Ephesians 1:11–13, the purpose of salvation is that we should be brought into a state in which we glorify God. A Christian is one who is increasingly able to glorify God, who is being fashioned by God so as to glorify him, both in the Christian's heart and also in this world as he or she performs his will and displays a God-like character. This is something Paul has been stressing throughout, that our salvation—our forgiveness and redemption, our election and adoption—is not an end but a means. There is a great end far above our salvation, namely, the glory of God. Therefore, D. Martyn Lloyd-Jones writes, "The essential proof of salvation . . . is that the supreme object and ambition of the Christian's life now is to live to the glory of God."[2] The Christian is one who actively, willingly, joyfully promotes God's glory. We are advancing in Christianity precisely to the extent that this can be said of us.

HEIRS AND GOD'S INHERITANCE

In this passage, Paul emphasizes three things about God's plan as it deals with us. Ephesians 1:11 begins, "In him we have obtained an inheritance." The Greek verb here is *klēroō,* which means "choose by lot," with the idea of inheritance in mind. Many scholars argue that since this verb is passive here, it is better yet translated that we have "been made an inheritance." So Paul means either that we have become heirs of God or that we have become God's inheritance. In Ephesians 1:14, Paul speaks of the Holy Spirit as a guarantee of "our inheritance," which argues for the former view. But Ephesians 1:13 says we are marked with a seal by the Spirit, which speaks of God's marking his possession, which argues for the latter view. Therefore, it seems that the best way to handle Paul's use of this term is to consider both perspectives.

According to God's plan, Christians are heirs of God. This idea takes us back to the example of Old Testament Israel. Upon entering the Promised Land, all tribes and families received their allotted portion of land on which to live. Together they inherited the land of blessing and each had their own portion, distributed by lot. Likewise, Christians have a place in the eternal provision of heaven. Furthermore, we remember the special status of the priestly tribe of Levi. Unlike the other tribes, the priests received no allotment of land. Rather, their inheritance was the Lord: "The LORD is his inheritance" (Deut. 10:9). This idea carries over to Christians, who are a kingdom of priests (1 Peter 2:9). Romans 8:17 says that if we are "children, then [we are] heirs—heirs of God and fellow heirs with Christ, provided we suffer with him in order that we may also be glorified with him." As co-heirs we will own everything with Jesus, indeed, we will share in God's glory in mutual possession in Christ.

We are heirs of God, and ultimately it is himself that God bequeaths to us. He is our inheritance. We possess God by knowing him, and we will have an ever-increasing possession of God for eternity future, beginning now. We possess God as our own by loving him, by trusting him, by praising him and in all these ways he gives us his own heart in return. Like the Shekinah glory cloud dwelling within Israel, God lives in us, as he moves and empowers us to reflect and partake of his glory.

At the same time, we are his inheritance. God said to Israel: "The LORD has taken you and brought you out of the iron furnace, out of Egypt, to be a people of his own inheritance, as you are this day" (Deut. 4:20). "The LORD's portion is his people, Jacob his allotted heritage" (Deut. 32:9).

These two come together in the great promise of God's covenant. In Hebrews 8:10 the Lord says, "I will be their God, and they will be my people." We are to know God and be known of him, to love God and to be loved by him in covenant marriage, to glorify God and share his glory as co-heirs with his Son, Jesus Christ. That is our high destiny in Christ, our extraordinary privilege, and if we are truly aware of it we will surely make this relationship with God the chief pursuit of our lives.

In an extraordinary essay, *The Weight of Glory,* C. S. Lewis points to this as the fulfillment of our deepest and highest longing. He says that we now possess a portion of God's glory through what we see in nature; for instance, the beauty of a sunrise is there for us to see if we only get up early enough. He then comments, "But we want so much more. . . . We do not want merely to see beauty, though, God knows, even that is bounty enough. We want something else which can hardly be put into words—to be united with the beauty we see, to pass into it, to receive it into ourselves, to bathe in it, to become part of it." That is what God has planned for us. As Lewis summarizes, "The leaves of the New Testament are rustling with the rumor [that we will put on glory], that greater glory of which Nature is only the first sketch."[3]

JEWS AND GENTILES RECONCILED IN CHRIST

The second insight Paul provides regarding God's glorious plan has to do with the fulfillment of his covenant purpose. This comes through in terms of the Jews and the Gentiles, each in succession becoming God's people through union with Jesus Christ. Neither of these is mentioned explicitly, but they are implicit in the way that Paul speaks of "we," "you," and "us." Speaking of Jews, he says that "we who were the first to hope in Christ might be to the praise of his glory." Speaking of his Gentile readers he adds, "In him you also, when you heard the word of truth, the gospel of your salvation, and believed in him, were sealed with the promised Holy Spirit."

Ephesians 1:11 thus speaks in a restrictive sense; it is Paul's *we*—Christian Jews—who fulfilled the Old Testament statements of Israel as God's inheritance. God had promised that Israel would be his portion, and it was ultimately in the believing Jews that this was fulfilled. Paul argues this way elsewhere, such as in Romans 11, that God did not abandon his promises to the Jews because many Christians, like Paul himself, were Jews. "I ask, then," he writes, "has God rejected his people? By no means! For I myself am an Israelite, a descendant of Abraham, a member of the tribe of Benjamin" (Rom. 11:1).

Therefore, it is "we who were the first to hope in Christ," Christian Jews, who fulfill God's purpose. But Paul is not proposing Jewish superiority in the church, because this also became true of the Gentile believers when they were included in Christ. The key to all this is "in Christ." It is Jesus Christ who fulfills the promise of Old Testament Israel; it is Jesus who is the portion of the heavenly Father. The believing Jews became God's inheritance in the same way the Gentiles did, namely, "in him," which is how Ephesians 1:11 begins, that is, by hoping in, believing in, Jesus Christ and his gospel. It is in Christ that we become heirs of God and his possession, for, as Paul elsewhere writes, "For all the promises of God find their Yes in him" (2 Cor. 1:20).

God's glorious plan first worked through the Jews as the remnant hoped in Christ. God then used them—Jewish evangelists and apostles like Paul—to preach the gospel for the inclusion of the Gentiles. This fulfilled the great promise spoken to Abraham so long before: "I will make of you a great nation, and I will bless you . . . in you all the families of the earth shall be blessed" (Gen. 12:2–3). This also introduces a theme Paul will expound in Ephesians 2, the working of peace on earth by reconciling all the peoples into one new humanity in Jesus Christ. Charles Hodge explains:

> The purpose of God is to bring all the subjects of redemption into one harmonious body. . . . This purpose is realized in the conversion of the Jewish Christians . . . and . . . the Gentile Christians, to whom his epistle is specially addressed, are comprehended in the same purpose. . . . Both Jews and Gentiles are, by the mediation of Christ, and in union with him, brought to be partakers of the benefits of that plan of mercy which

God had purposed in himself, and which he has now revealed for the salvation of men.[4]

So great a salvation, bringing about the peace on earth that humankind has failed to achieve apart from God, is surely to the praise of God's glory. Our world knows only the peace brought about by external means, either through force or enticement. But the peace of Christ is inward and spiritual. It eliminates the division. It takes people who have been conscious of their differences—those of race or education or class or nationality—and gives them a new unity through union with Jesus Christ. We become something new together in Christ. This is God's plan for human reconciliation, and it has vast implications for the church. James Montgomery Boice comments:

> I am sorry for churches made up of one class of people, as many American churches are, for they lack opportunity to show this new unification of people effectively. Church growth specialists tell us that this is the best way for churches to grow, people being most attracted to those who are like themselves, and it may be so. . . . But at what cost is this growth purchased! I would rather have less growth and more glory given to Christ. I would rather have small totals but a larger body in the sense of a larger number of the types and conditions of people who are included in it.[5]

BY GRACE, THROUGH FAITH

God's glorious plan brings praise to him by making us heirs of God and also God's inheritance, bringing Jews and Gentiles together in Jesus Christ. The third thing Paul notes about God's plan is that salvation is entered into by faith in the gospel of Jesus Christ. He says this about Jews and Gentiles; the former were "the first to hope in Christ," and the latter were included in Christ when they heard and believed "the word of truth, the gospel of your salvation." Paul makes no mention of works or merits but only faith in Christ.

If we think about this, we will recognize the genius of this design. God's plan is directed to giving glory to God alone. God's way of salvation must therefore be able to incorporate us into Christ without detracting glory from God. The way this is accomplished is by salvation through faith alone. Paul explains in Romans 4:16, "That is why it depends on faith, in order that the promise may rest on grace." Faith is something we do, but it is not a work. Faith is God's gift through the Holy Spirit, a point Paul makes in Ephesians 2:8–9, "For by grace you have been saved through faith. And this is not your own doing; it is the gift of God, not a result of works, so that no one may boast." By faith you are actively involved in your relationship to God, you are called to "work out your own salvation with fear and trembling," but only because "it is God who works in you, both to will and to work for his good pleasure" (Phil. 2:12–13). Therefore, faith is a way for us to be joined to Jesus Christ for salvation, but a way in which God alone is glorified, because faith is the result of his grace working in us.

Ephesians 1:13 implies a helpful definition of faith: "You also, when you heard the word of truth, the gospel of your salvation, and believed in him, were sealed with the promised Holy Spirit." We are going to consider the sealing of the Spirit in the next chapter, but for now we can observe that faith is believing the message of the gospel. The gospel is the good news of Jesus Christ, the proclamation of what Jesus did and its saving implications. It includes historical fact and doctrine. It is not enough to believe that Jesus died, but that he died for our sins. It is not even enough to believe he rose from the dead; we must believe he was raised as our Lord, God having accepted

136

his sacrifice and appointed him as the means of our justification. Thus Paul writes in Romans 4:25, "[Jesus] was delivered up for our trespasses and raised for our justification." Faith means believing the saving truth in Jesus Christ, receiving him as our Lord and Savior, and committing ourselves to him.

God's plan called for salvation through faith in every era since the fall. This is how the Jews were saved of old. Paul stresses, for instance, that long before Moses and the law, Abraham was saved by faith and not by works. Paul says in Galatians 3:6–9, "Abraham believed God, and it was counted to him as righteousness . . . . So then, those who are of faith are blessed along with Abraham, the man of faith." In Paul's day believing Jews were saved by faith, being "the first to hope in Christ," and Gentiles were also incorporated into Christ by means of faith in his gospel they had heard.

This being the case, Christians must proclaim the gospel! This must be our message, not self-help methods, not political agendas, but Christ crucified and raised from the dead. In 1 Corinthians 15:3–4 Paul says of his own ministry, "For I delivered to you as of first importance what I also received: that Christ died for our sins in accordance with the Scriptures, that he was buried, that he was raised on the third day in accordance with the Scriptures." In Romans he says, "If you confess with your mouth that Jesus is Lord and believe in your heart that God raised him from the dead, you will be saved. . . . For the Scripture says, 'Everyone who believes in him will not be put to shame'" (Rom. 10:9–13). That prompts Paul to ask the Christians, "But how are they to call on him in whom they have not believed? And how are they to believe in him of whom they have never heard? And how are they to hear without someone preaching? And how are they to preach unless they are sent? As it is written, 'How beautiful are the feet of those who preach the good news!'" (Rom. 10:14–15). Surely those are questions for the church to ponder today, when so many other messages crowd out the gospel of Christ's death and resurrection, by which alone men and women can be saved.

God has a plan for our salvation in which he is utterly sovereign. Yet he has decreed the necessity of faith. This passage shows the highest view of God's sovereignty fully at home with the need for evangelism. People say, "If God is sovereign in salvation, then why bother preaching and witnessing?" Our answer is that we must evangelize because God is sovereign and his plan calls for belief in the gospel as the means by which men and women are saved. God brings people into Jesus Christ through faith in "the word of truth, the gospel of your salvation." It is only through faith in Christ that God's sovereign election is revealed in the lives of individuals. John Calvin put it this way:

> How do we know that God has elected us before the creation of the world? By believing in Jesus Christ. . . . Whosoever then believes is thereby assured that God has worked in him, and faith is, as it were, the duplicate copy that God gives us of the original of our adoption. God has his eternal counsel, and he always reserves to himself the chief and original record of which he gives us a copy by faith.[6]

This means that you can be part of God's saving plan, you can be one of his cherished people, whoever you are, wherever you come from, whatever you have done, if you will believe that Jesus died for your sins and rose to be your Lord and Savior. If you will trust in him, you will be able to know that God's eternal love has been set upon you.

THE POTTER'S HANDS

John Stott concludes his study of these verses by describing what he calls "a clash of wills" whenever people first encounter the biblical teaching of God's total sovereignty in salvation. He says:

> Such Christian talk comes into violent collision with the man-centredness and self-centredness of the world. Fallen man, imprisoned in his own little ego, has an almost boundless confidence in the power of his own will, and an almost insatiable appetite for the praise of his own glory. But the people of God have at least begun to be turned inside out. The new society has new values and new ideals. For God's people are God's possession who live by God's will and for God's glory.[7]

People dislike the Bible's imagery of God as the potter, fashioning and shaping us according to his purpose and will. They find it oppressive that God exercises such sovereignty over our destinies. But for those of us who know God, who have come to know his love in Jesus Christ, the feel of the potter's hands upon the rim of our lives is not a cause for resentment but rather for joy. If you come to know this God, this sovereign potter, through Jesus Christ, then you will come to trust him, to love him, to delight in the hand of his providence as it shapes and moves your life. You will realize that in all things God is working for your good (Rom. 8:28), that in his hands we "are being transformed into [his] image from one degree of glory to another" (2 Cor. 3:18).

If you resent the hand of God shaping your life, then let me encourage you to look at that hand. What you will see there is the mark of nails that pierced the flesh of Jesus Christ; you will see the marks of God's love for you that took up the cross, dying in your place, "the righteous for the unrighteous, that he might bring us to God" (1 Peter 3:18).

At the center of God's glorious plan is the cross of Jesus Christ, where God's love for sinners is revealed in the highest.

It was God's will that humanity should have the skill to fashion iron into hammer and nails; it was God's plan that humanity should take wood from the tree and make it into the shape of a cross. Donald Grey Barnhouse writes:

> The Lord will allow man to take hold of Him and bring Him to that cross; He will stretch out His hands to that cross, and in so doing will take the sins of man upon Himself and make it possible for those who have despised and rejected Him to come unto Him and know the joy of sins removed and forgiven, to know the assurance of pardon and eternal life, and to enter into the prospect of the hope of glory with Him forever. This is even our God, and there is none like unto Him.[8]

That is the hand that presses upon the clay of your life, fashioning you into something glorious according to his sovereign plan. It is also the hand that beckons you to come, to hear the gospel and believe, thereby joining the throng of those in Christ who have become heirs of God and God's precious possession, partaking of his glory and praising him forever. Amen.

11

MARKED WITH
A SEAL

Ephesians 1:13

*In him you also, when you heard the word
of truth, the gospel of your salvation, and believed in him,
were sealed with the promised Holy Spirit.*
—Ephesians 1:13

*J*ohn Bunyan's classic allegory, *Pilgrim's Progress*, tells of
Christian's journey from the City of Destruction to the
Celestial City, representing heaven. After many difficulties and
dangers, Christian finally arrives at the gates with the bells joyfully
ringing. There he presents the certificate he had earlier received
and that promised him entry. The document is carried to the King,
who inspects it for authenticity. After it is approved, Christian is
allowed entry into the shining city for an eternity of happiness.[1]

This is a scenario envisioned by Paul in his letter to the Ephesians. In Ephesians 1:13 he says, "When you heard the word of truth, the gospel of your salvation, and believed in him, [you] were sealed with the promised Holy Spirit." The seal he mentions is the kind embossed on an official document to validate its authenticity, like that which we find on a passport or birth certificate today, and like the one Christian presented at the gate to the Celestial City. Without the seal the document cannot be accepted, but with the seal it must be.

Paul turns to this at a point of transition in his three-part hymn of praise to God for his blessings in salvation. Already he spoke of God the Father ordaining our salvation in sovereign grace. Next, he wrote of God the Son accomplishing the work of our salvation through his blood. Now he turns our thoughts to the work of the Spirit, who applies to us what Christ has achieved, here sealing us as God's cherished possession.

MARKED WITH A SEAL

The last chapter showed that Ephesians 1:11–12 summarizes all that has gone before. These verses speak of God's glorious plan in which we are saved by faith, becoming God's cherished people and his heirs. Paul continues with that thought, especially picking up the idea that we are God's portion and possession. Since we belong to God, he marks us with a seal. In Paul's day, a prominent person would choose an emblem as his official seal. Using melted wax, he affixed an imprint of this emblem to an object he wanted to identify as belonging to or coming from him. In this same way Paul speaks of God's identifying all who belong to him in Christ.

Charles Hodge points out three purposes of a seal. First, a seal is used to authenticate or confirm something as genuine and true, as with the seal on a passport or other document. In this way the Holy Spirit authenticates professing Christians as genuine. Second, a seal marks an object as one's property. Today, we brand cattle and other livestock; in Paul's day slaves were similarly marked, as were other kinds of possessions. Third, a seal renders something secure. A seal was placed on Jesus' tomb after his crucifixion to keep the body from being taken. Likewise, believers are protected by the seal of the Holy Spirit. We are authenticated and thus assured of God's saving blessing; we are marked as belonging to him; and we are secured and protected against those things that would threaten to separate us from God.[2]

There was good reason for this teaching to have special meaning to the Ephesian church, as we learn in Acts 19. When Paul first came to Ephesus, he met some disciples and for some reason doubted their Christianity. He asked them if they had received the Holy Spirit when they believed. They replied that they knew nothing of the Spirit, so Paul inquired further. The men knew only John's baptism, that is, the testimony of John the Baptist that the awaited Messiah was soon to come. Paul taught them about Jesus, and they believed in the gospel and were baptized. Acts 19:6 says, "When Paul had laid his hands on them, the Holy Spirit came on them, and they began speaking in tongues and prophesying." The point was not that believers have to speak in tongues; the charismatic gifts were but a sign of the Spirit in that epochal age. The point was that in response to their faith in Christ, the men received the indwelling Holy Spirit. Here was an extension of the once-for-all outpouring of the Spirit at Pentecost to these distant people in Asia Minor. The coming of the Spirit validated their profession of faith as true and marked them as God's new covenant people.

In what manner, then, does the Spirit seal Christians? Jesus' statement in John 3:8 warns us against trying to see the Spirit. Comparing the Spirit with the wind, he says, "You hear its sound, but you do not know where it comes from." The

point is that the Spirit is known only by his effects. You feel
and observe tangible evidence, and that tells you the wind has
blown. Paul, for instance, speaks of the "fruit of the Spirit,"
tangible manifestations of the Spirit's presence through our
growth in godly character. "The fruit of the Spirit," Paul writes,
"is love, joy, peace, patience, kindness, goodness, faithfulness,
gentleness, self-control" (Gal. 5:22–23). When you see these
things, in your own life or in another's, you can be confident
that the one professing to be a Christian really is one. By the
Spirit's work in producing this fruit we are also kept safe in
the faith. Outwardly, this is how the Spirit works as a seal. Inwardly, Paul says in Romans 8:16, "The Spirit himself bears witness with our spirit that we are children of God." In these
ways—by the tangible evidence of the Spirit's fruit in our lives
and by his ministry to our souls—the Spirit marks us as those
who belong to God and are kept safe for salvation by his power.

In our verse Paul says two things about the Spirit that
guide us further. Literally, he writes of "the Spirit of promise."
This is the Spirit of God who was promised and through whom
the promises of salvation are fulfilled in Christ. On the day of
Pentecost, when the ascended Lord Jesus poured out the Spirit
on the church, Peter explained what was happening as the fulfillment of Joel 2:28–32. The point of that prophecy was that
when the Messiah came and accomplished his work, he would
pour out the Spirit on his people. As a result, people would
know God and be saved by calling on his name. This is indeed
how the Spirit works, revealing God to our hearts and placing
the cry of faith on our lips, both marking us and securing our
salvation. Leon Morris thus says the promised Spirit "is the
guarantee that all God's promises will be fulfilled in the believer."[3]

Paul also calls the Spirit "holy." The construction of this
verse seems to emphasize this point: literally, Paul writes of
"the Spirit of promise, the Holy One." How do we know, then,

that someone is indwelt by the Spirit and thus marked as belonging to God? Through holiness. Through godly character and actions and habits. Through evidence of sanctification. Hodge puts this all together, writing, "This, then, is the great gift which Christ secures for his people, the in-dwelling of the Holy Spirit, as the source of truth, holiness, consolation and eternal life."[4]

DISTINGUISHING MARKS OF THE HOLY SPIRIT

Let's make this practical. Is it possible for us to know that we are saved and that we will get into heaven when we die? Can we credibly, if not perfectly, identify others as true believers? Our verse answers both of these in the affirmative, because God sends the Spirit to seal all who are his own, and the Spirit is identified by tangible, observable effects of his indwelling presence.

Understanding this is important when dealing with new converts. Someone makes profession of faith in Christ. What is it that proves the reality of that profession? The answer is evidence of the Holy Spirit. This is especially key in times of revival and mass conversions, when God is bringing many people to faith, and even more so in the context of revivalistic efforts, which so often rely on manipulative efforts to get people to walk down an aisle or pray a certain prayer.

One person who was greatly concerned about this was Jonathan Edwards, when in 1734 his church in Northampton, Massachusetts, experienced revival. Edwards realized that some people were coming under a general spiritual influence without truly being saved. He wanted to discern false conversions and to defend true conversions against those who questioned the revival. He wrote an important book dealing with these matters, *The Distinguishing Marks of a Work of the Spirit of God*. His theme verse was 1 John 4:1: "Beloved, do not believe every spirit, but test the spirits to see whether they are from God."

Edwards approached the subject from two perspectives. First, he pointed out signs that should not be confused with a real work of the Holy Spirit, noting that in times of great spiritual commotion much excitement may be a sign of psychological stress or even counterfeits of true conversion brought about by the devil. In this regard, he spoke of physical or emotional excitement, which may accompany a true work of the Spirit but often happens when no real converting work has taken place. He spoke this way of bodily effects in general, "such as tears, trembling, groans, loud outcries, agonies of the body, or the failing of bodily strength."[5] Edwards warned not to confuse external excitement with inward spiritual change. He would not consider someone to be converted simply because he raised his hand or because she walked down an aisle or prayed a prayer as coached by a preacher, much less because he became overwrought with emotion. Those things often happen when someone is converted, but they are not proof of a genuine work of the Holy Spirit. They themselves are not the mark with which God seals his own.

What, then, are the distinguishing marks of a true work of the Holy Spirit? Edwards listed five, and I think they are helpful for us as true signs of the Spirit's work, genuine evidences that show that we are sealed unto God. First is the elevation of esteem in Jesus Christ as the Son of God and Savior. This is the single surest sign of the true operation of the Holy Spirit. "He will bear witness about me," Jesus said of the Spirit (John 15:26); "He will glorify me" (John 16:14). False spirituality isn't interested in Jesus but is focused on self and on the excitement of what is taking place. But a true work of the Spirit exalts Jesus Christ and leads us to faith and love for him. Second, a true work of the Spirit opposes the reign of Satan and causes us to turn from sin. Mere moralism does not prove the

Spirit's work, but Christ-exalting sanctification is always a sign of his presence. Third, a true conversion brings an increase of interest in God's Word, a desire to know what the Bible teaches and to put it into practice. Fourth is a sound grasp of true doctrine and a zeal to defend it against attacks. People who come to love sound teaching, who reject worldly and secular humanistic tenets, are evidently under the influence of God's Holy Spirit. Fifth is the mark of love. Edwards writes, "If the spirit that is at work among a people operates as a spirit of love to God and man, it is a sure sign that it is the Spirit of God."[6]

An exaltation of Jesus Christ, repentance from sin, interest in God's Word, and a grasp of sound teaching, all coupled with a new love for God and for others. These are sure proofs of the Holy Spirit, marking us as God's own. It is as he works in these ways, deepening our relationship with God, that the Spirit is called by Paul "the Spirit of adoption as sons, by whom we cry, 'Abba! Father!'" (Rom. 8:15).

But what if there is only imperfect evidence of these things? We exalt Christ, but not nearly so much as we should. We hate sin, but we still sin. We love the Bible but often neglect it. Our sound doctrine bears too little influence on our lives. We love others, but still there is the old, familiar love of self. Does that mean we may not really have the Spirit, that we may not be saved? If you understand the Bible's view of humankind's spiritual deadness in sin, then you realize that if we truly have any of these things—incompletely but genuinely—it can only be because of the Spirit's work. No Christian will be perfect in this life (see Phil. 3:12), but non-Christians will not bear these true marks of the Holy Spirit, especially when they are tested under trials.

Therefore, if we have trusted in Christ and can see imperfect but genuine evidence of the Spirit's work, we should not doubt our salvation. It is precisely because we have cause for doubt that God places his seal upon us. In heaven we will not have this need, for then we will be perfect and perfectly safe. It is because we have need of assurance now that God sends the Spirit to seal us; it is because we now are so weak and vulnerable and inconstant that we need the Spirit God so freely sends.

If you show sincere evidence of the Holy Spirit's work, bearing fruit through faith in Jesus Christ, you may be thus assured that you do belong to God and that his power is at work in you. This is important to Paul, who prays later in this chapter for us to know "the immeasurable greatness of [God's] power toward us who believe, according to the working of his great might that he worked in Christ when he raised him from the dead" (Eph. 1:19–20). With clear evidence of this Spirit's presence in your life through faith in Christ, you may be assured of your safety as God's own and cherished one.

THE HOLY SPIRIT AND FAITH

This verse also makes a telling statement about the relationship of faith to the gift of the Holy Spirit. Paul says, "When you . . . believed in him, [you] were sealed with the promised Holy Spirit." This says that the Holy Spirit's sealing work comes in response to our faith.

We know from elsewhere in the Scripture, however, that it is the Spirit's regenerating work that enables us to believe in the first place. Paul definitively states in 1 Corinthians 2:14, "The natural person does not accept the things of the Spirit of God, for they are folly to him, and he is not able to understand them because they are spiritually discerned." This means that the regenerating, enlightening work of the Holy Spirit precedes and causes faith.

But by writing this verse the way he did, Paul obviously wants to emphasize something other than the Spirit's initial regenerating work. John Calvin explains, "Besides our receiving of faith at the hand of the Holy Spirit and besides his enlightening of us by his grace . . . God also secures us in such a way that we do not fall away."[7] By faith we are joined to Christ, and from Christ comes the Spirit to seal us—to identify, authenticate, and secure us for salvation.

We need to realize that not only does our initial coming to faith depend on the Spirit, but henceforth our keeping the faith also relies on God's power and not our own. Calvin shows his pastoral insight when he writes of the same Spirit who first brought us to faith also working alongside our faith to keep us in the way of salvation:

> Let us notice how volatile men are. He that is best disposed to follow God will soon fall, for we are so frail that the devil will overcome us every minute of time, if God does not hold us up with a strong hand. . . . For if he did not fight for us, alas, what would become of us? We should be absolutely confounded, and not by reason of one stroke only, but there would be an infinite number of falls. . . . As soon as we were in the way of salvation, we should at once be turned out of it by our own frailty, lightness and inconstancy, if we were not restrained and if God did not so work in us that we might, by his Holy Spirit, overcome all the assaults of the devil and the world. [The] Spirit is pleased to abide in us and to give us perseverance, that we do not draw back in the midst of our way.[8]

If you are discouraged by your weakness and sin, this is a source for your confidence. In his first epistle, Peter says that "by God's power [you] are being guarded through faith for a salvation ready to be revealed in the last time" (1 Peter 1:5). Paul likewise spoke of the Spirit in Philippians 1:6, saying he is "sure of this, that he who began a good work in you will bring it to completion at the day of Jesus Christ."

SEALING AND THE DAY OF JUDGMENT

This idea of sealing is especially linked to our protection in the day of God's judgment, just as the lamb's blood marked the Israelite houses when the angel of death passed over on the eve of the Exodus. Ezekiel 9 also shows the link between God's mark and escape from his judgment. There, a great judgment falls upon the faithless people of Jerusalem, but first God sends his angel to place a seal on his faithful people: "Pass through the city, through Jerusalem," he says, "and put a mark on the foreheads of the men who sigh and groan over all the abominations that are committed in it" (Ezek. 9:4). Everyone who lacked God's mark was slaughtered in the judgment. This is how it will be in the end. Jesus warned us: "On that day many will say to me, 'Lord, Lord. . . . And then will I declare to them, 'I never knew you; depart from me, you workers of lawlessness'" (Matt. 7:22–23). It is only those who belong to God and are sealed by him who will be known and received by Christ in that day.

The same mark, however, that saves us from God's wrath to come creates the opposite effect in this present world. Being identified as belonging to Jesus will cause the world to hate you. Jesus said, "'A servant is not greater than his master.' If they persecuted me, they will also persecute you" (John 15:20).

This comes through forcefully in Revelation 13:16, where we are told that the Beast will coerce people to receive his mark on the hand or forehead. Everyone who does not have his seal will be persecuted. But Revelation 14:9–10 adds, "If anyone worships the beast and its image and receives a mark on his forehead or on his hand, he also will drink the wine of God's wrath." If we do not have God's mark of ownership, it is not as if we have no mark, that we therefore are not owned by anyone. You say you are your own man, your own woman, but if you do not have God's seal of ownership, you are owned and sealed by the world in rebellion to God. We are either marked by God and persecuted by the devil and the world, or marked by the world to be condemned in the day of God's judgment. Revelation 22:4 says of God's people in heaven, those who drink from the waters of life and eat from the tree of life, "they will see his face, and his name will be on their foreheads."

That being the case, there is nothing more important than that we should be "sealed for the day of redemption" (Eph. 4:30) by God's Spirit. We are either sealed by God, having believed on Christ and his gospel, or we are sealed by the world through sin and unbelief. Only those whose sins are cleansed by the blood of Christ and who are sealed by the Spirit will escape the wrath of God that is to come.

SEALED IN CHRIST

The kind of confidence Paul writes of here is something we need if we are going to grow in faith and godliness. It's not easy to turn from our sins, and this teaching about the Holy Spirit helps us. And yet it is not the Spirit to whom we must look to gain security, not to him we are to cry for the seal of God's blessing. Our verse says, "In him you . . . were sealed with the promised Holy Spirit," that is, in Jesus Christ. In the Greek, the words "in him" begin this sentence, just as they begin Ephesians 1:11, forming a deliberate parallel: "In him we have obtained an inheritance" (v. 11). "In him you also . . . were sealed" (v. 13).

That means that if you lack assurance, it is to Jesus Christ that you must turn, for it is in him that you are sealed for the final redemption. If you feel condemned for your sin, "the blood of Jesus . . . cleanses us from all sin" (1 John 1:7). If you seek to have your salvation validated, it is Jesus who says, "Every-

151

MARKED WITH A SEAL

one who acknowledges me before men, I also will acknowledge before my Father who is in heaven" (Matt. 10:32). If you seek power in your weakness, Jesus promised, "Because I live, you also will live" (John 14:19). He adds, in Hebrews 13:5–6, "'I will never leave you nor forsake you.' So we can confidently say, 'The Lord is my helper; I will not fear; what can man do to me?'"

In *Pilgrim's Progress,* Bunyan's hero enters the Celestial City having presented his valid and sealed certificate of acceptance. But where did he get it? Bunyan gets it right, because he tells us Christian had been staggering along with a great burden on his back, the weight of his sin, when at last he came upon a cross. "He ran until he came to a peak where a cross stood; a little below, in the bottom, was a tomb. When Christian reached the cross, his burden became loose, fell from his back, and tumbled into the tomb. I never saw the burden again." That is what happens to everyone who comes in faith to the cross of Christ—the weight of your guilt falls away, having been paid by his precious blood. But something else happened as Christian stood there weeping at the cross. Bunyan tells us:

> Three Shining Ones approached and greeted him. "Peace," the first said, "Your sins are forgiven" (Mk. 2:5). The second removed his filthy rags and dressed him in rich clothing (Zech. 3:4). The third put a mark on his forehead (Eph. 1:13) and gave him a sealed roll. He told Christian to look at the roll as he ran and to leave it at the celestial gate.[9]

There is the complete salvation for all who come to Jesus Christ in faith. We are forgiven our sins, clothed in the righteous robes of Christ, and sealed for salvation by the promised Holy Spirit. In Romans 5:1–5, Paul puts together all these blessings that are ours in Christ, whoever we are and whatever we have done, if we come believing to the cross: "Since we have been justified by faith, we have peace with God through our Lord Jesus Christ. . . . And we rejoice in hope of the glory of God . . . because God's love has been poured into our hearts through the Holy Spirit who has been given to us." All that can be yours if you will come to him in faith. All that is already yours if you are in Christ, so that now you may live for him who gave himself for you.

12

THE DEPOSIT OF
OUR INHERITANCE

Ephesians 1:14

*Who is the guarantee of our inheritance until
we acquire possession of it, to the praise of his glory.*
—Ephesians 1:14

According to author James R. White, the Trinity is
the forgotten doctrine of Christianity. He argues:

Most Christian people have forgotten the central place
the doctrine is to hold in the Christian life. It is rarely
the topic of sermons and Bible studies, rarely the object of adoration and worship. . . . The doctrine is mis-
understood as well as ignored . . . it does not hold the
place it should in the proclamation of the Gospel mes-

sage, nor in the life of the individual believer in prayer, worship, and service.[1]

That could not be said about the apostle Paul, who structured his whole approach to Christian salvation around the Trinity. This great opening section of Ephesians, which we conclude in this chapter, offers praise to God for the blessings each divine person of the Trinity contributes to our salvation, which therefore rests on an unshakeable foundation.

The Trinity is perhaps Christianity's highest and greatest mystery. The Bible presents the one God in three persons. As the Westminster Larger Catechism explains, they are "the same in substance, equal in power and glory; although distinguished by their personal properties" (Q. 9). Understanding how the three persons work together answers many of our concerns regarding the stability of our salvation. How can salvation fail us, when it was ordained by God the Father before there even was time? Before creation happened, before any of the circumstances that threaten us were even possible, before our sin and weakness even came into existence, God decided that we should be saved as his holy children. The triumph of Christ's saving work likewise gives us assurance. How can sin condemn us when Christ has paid its penalty? How can God's law assail us if Jesus has fulfilled it for us? How will the flesh, the world, or the devil destroy us while Christ now reigns in power, interceding for us in heaven?

Yet still there is need for the work of God the Spirit. How can I be included in this salvation? How can I know these things are not merely true in the abstract but true for me? I see there is a sure salvation, but how do I know that I am one of those saved? The answer is in the work of God the Spirit, who enters us into Christ by faith, thus to receive the benefits of this Triune saving work. The Bible says a cord of three strands is not easily broken (Eccles. 4:12); in the Trinity we have an unbreakable redemption in which we may rest secure.

That is why White began his book by writing, "I love the Trinity"—speaking both of God and of the doctrine.[2] Paul loved the Trinity, too, and that is why this great doxology focuses on the work of God in his three persons. The God displayed in Trinity is a God of unfathomable glory, and a God who meets our every need. If anyone asks you, therefore, how you consider your salvation to be secure, you may point to the Trinity. Our salvation rests on the sovereign authority of God the Father, on the finished work of God the Son, and on the personal relationship provided by God the Holy Spirit.

THE AGE OF THE SPIRIT

Our present verse focuses on the Holy Spirit, who in at least one specific sense is the most important person for us in the Godhead. I say this because the Spirit is the only divine person whose primary contribution to our salvation is expressed in the present tense. All three persons of the Godhead are involved in every aspect of our salvation—past, present, and future. But the decisive contributions made by God the Father and God the Son are in the past, even though their present work is essential. The Father ordained us. Christ died and rose again. All this is done. But in the work of the Spirit we now turn from the past tense to the present. The Father ordained; the Son accomplished; but God the Spirit applies salvation. The Spirit was always involved in our redemption, but it is now that he steps to the fore, as it were, so that this present age between the first and second comings of Christ is rightly called the age of the Spirit.

In the previous chapter I mentioned John Bunyan's *Pilgrim's Progress,* the allegory that follows Christian through his many dangers and difficulties until he arrives safe at the Celestial City. It is to the challenges of this present life that the Holy Spirit's work is especially directed. It is the Spirit, on behalf of the Father and the Son, who comes to lead us through the Slough of Despond, up the Hill of Difficulty, out of Vanity Fair, and past Doubting Castle. It is the Spirit who empowers our perseverance and keeps us in the faith. In Ephesians 1:14, Paul adds that he "is the guarantee of our inheritance until we acquire possession of it."

From time to time in these studies of Ephesians I have asked, "What is a Christian?" This, too, may be expressed in terms of the Trinity. Ephesians 1:5 tells us that a Christian is a child of God the Father, since "he predestined us for adoption" as his sons. In Ephesians 1:7 we learned that a Christian is a sinner who has been redeemed by the blood of God the Son, our Lord Jesus Christ. We now find that a Christian is one who has received the Holy Spirit, who seals us for salvation and guarantees our full redemption.

The Holy Spirit is not an add-on for upper-level Christians. When Paul says, in Ephesians 1:13, that "when you heard the word of truth, the gospel of your salvation, and believed in him, [you] were sealed with the promised Holy Spirit," he does not mean that first comes saving faith and then, sometime later and perhaps only for a special few, comes the Holy Spirit. Paul means, as Robert Reymond explains, "Faith in Christ is the instrumental cause of the sealing. That is to say, the moment one trusts in Christ, *that same moment* the Holy Spirit seals him in Christ."[3] Paul speaks of the promised Holy Spirit, recalling that the Old Testament looked forward to his outpouring in the day of the Messiah. Jeremiah predicted, "They shall all know me, from the least of them to the greatest" (Jer. 31:34). Since the Spirit is poured out on all those who belong to God, it is not possible to be a Christian without receiving the Holy Spirit.

Therefore the question is, "Have you received the Holy

Spirit?" In the last chapter we examined a number of marks of the Spirit, but now I want to narrow them down to the one great mark of the Holy Spirit, namely, saving faith in Jesus Christ. Handley Moule says of the Spirit, "His theme, His burden, is Jesus Christ. [His work] is to take of the things of Christ, to deal with . . . the finished work and inexhaustible riches of Christ, and . . . to manifest them to the spirit of man. It is to bring man, by a divine but inscrutable operation, to believe in Christ and to possess Him." What shows the presence of the Spirit in your life is not a fascination with the Spirit or with spirituality as such, but a fascination with Jesus Christ, a reliance on his work and a passion for his kingdom. Moule concludes, "The Spirit lies hidden as it were behind Christ Jesus," so that the Spirit is most in evidence when Christ is exalted.[4]

THE SPIRIT AS GUARANTEE

In Ephesians 1:13–14 Paul describes the Holy Spirit's work in applying salvation to our souls. First is the Spirit's sealing work, as he identifies, authenticates, and protects those who belong to God. In Ephesians 1:14, Paul expands our understanding, adding that the Spirit is "the guarantee of our inheritance." We belong to God, and so he marks us. But we also possess him as heirs, and he therefore gives the Spirit as the deposit of all that someday will be ours.

Paul describes the Spirit here with the Greek word *arrabōn*. This was the down payment paid at the time of a purchase, guaranteeing that the full amount would follow. According to the English Standard Version, Paul writes of the coming day when we will "acquire possession of it," that is, of our final salvation. But since Paul uses a form of the word *apolutrōsis*, which means "redemption," the New King James Version renders this better, saying that the Spirit is our guarantee "until the redemption of the purchased possession." Paul is pointing to the coming of Christ when all things, including our salvation, will be brought to consummation. In Luke 21:27–28, Jesus spoke of his future return, saying, "Then they will see the Son of Man coming in a cloud with power and great glory. Now when these things begin to take place, straighten up and raise your heads, because your redemption is drawing near." Paul refers to our redemption in that same way, pointing to the full fruition of what has already been established and begun at the cross of Christ.

Those who have come to Christ belong to God. The fullness of that relationship is yet to come, but God has made the down payment that secures the whole. If we have the Spirit, through faith in Christ, this guarantees that we will be in heaven, we will one day know the fullness of blessings that God intends for those who are his own.

Paul uses this word *arrabōn* two other times in his letters. The first is 2 Corinthians 1:22. There, Paul is speaking about the confidence we can have in present difficulties, since it is God who makes us stand firm. He explains, "He . . . has also put his seal on us and given us his Spirit in our hearts as a guarantee." The life of faith is hard, and many who call themselves Christians will not make good on their profession. What, then, is our assurance, especially when we learn how little we can trust our spiritual resources? Our assurance is the presence of the Holy Spirit, who marks us as God's own and guarantees our perseverance. Just as when we make a down payment on a home, so that an advance on the full amount guarantees our ownership, God secures our full redemption by the giving of his Holy Spirit. The Spirit's presence serves, as one writer puts is, as "the indisputable proof of God's determination to honor all the obligations he has assumed towards us under the covenant of grace."[5]

The other use of this term is in 2 Corinthians 5, where Paul is looking forward to the day when his earthly form will be exchanged for a heavenly body. He tires of the burdens of earthly life and looks forward to the journey's end. Speaking of this future glory, he adds, "He who has prepared us for this very thing is God, who has given us the Spirit as a guarantee" (2 Cor. 5:5). This means, as Donald Grey Barnhouse says, "We are not only saved, we are also safe. Christ paid the price of our sins, and the Holy Spirit maintains us in our sure position as children of God."[6]

THE SPIRIT AS FORETASTE

An important feature of the *arrabōn,* the down payment, is that it is paid in kind. We are going to buy a house with money, so we write a check as the deposit, which secures the property with an advance of money. In the same way, the gift of the Spirit is a foretaste of what God will give us in immeasurably greater extent upon the completion of our salvation.

Ephesians 1:14 describes the Spirit as the deposit of our inheritance. We are heirs of God. Just as he possesses us, we are to possess him. "I will be their God," he says repeatedly, "and they will be my people." By the Spirit we begin this mutual possession of love. We begin to enjoy our inheritance.

In his novel *The Testament,* John Grisham tells of a multibillionaire who kills himself moments after signing his final will. His worthless, loveless, and greedy children eagerly await the date when the will is to be read and executed. In the meantime they immediately start a spending spree, buying fabulous houses and luxury cars. But to their shock, they find that the entire fortune was bequeathed to a half-sister no one had ever heard of, a Christian missionary living far off in a jungle, and destitution stared them in the face.[7]

Christians are not like that when it comes to the riches of God's redemption. We are not waiting to see what if anything will come to us. God has publicly ordained and declared what will be given to all his children and heirs in Jesus Christ in the age to come. Paul says in 1 Corinthians 15:53, "This perishable body must put on the imperishable, and this mortal body must put on immortality." He adds in 2 Corinthians 5:1, "We have a building from God, a house not made with hands, eternal in the heavens." The apostle John, in his first epistle, can scarcely imagine what this will all be like. But what he does know fills him with wonder: "Beloved, we are God's children now, and what we will be has not yet appeared; but we know that when he appears we will be like him, because we shall see him as he is" (1 John 3:2). His vision in Revelation 22:3–5 vividly pictures the glory of which we now are heirs:

> No longer will there be anything accursed, but the throne of God and of the Lamb will be in it, and his servants will worship him. They will see his face, and his name will be on their foreheads. And night will be no more. They will need no light of lamp or sun, for the Lord God will be their light, and they will reign forever and ever.

These things are sure. They are not just a dim possibility if the will is found in our favor. The documents are all signed and sealed. They have been made public and are held in trust until the day of their execution, when the exalted Lord Jesus will step forward to open the seals and bring all things to consummation. We are heirs with our fortune held securely in trust. And just as many such heirs receive a generous allowance from the vast sum held in trust for them, so we are given the Spirit, who is the foretaste and firstfruit of all that remains to come. John Owen writes, "By the Holy Spirit, then, we get a foretaste of the fullness of that glory which God has prepared for those that love him and the more communion we have with the Holy Spirit as an 'earnest' the more we taste of that heavenly glory that awaits us."[8]

This reality was symbolized in Old Testament Israel with the offering of the firstfruits. When the harvest first came in, the people held a festival, rejoicing and thanking God for the fullness that soon would come. Paul uses this same expression regarding the resurrection of Jesus Christ. "Christ has been raised from the dead, the firstfruits of those who have fallen asleep" (1 Cor. 15:20). His resurrection is the beginning of our resurrection. In principle, since he is raised, we are raised with him, which is why Paul often refers to us in Ephesians as belonging "in the heavenly places." We are joined to Christ through faith and thus to his resurrection, the firstfruits of which come back to us through the giving of the Spirit. This guarantees our resurrection and glorification and provides us a portion of the life that then will be ours in full.

OUR PRESENT RICHES

This tells us that Christians have great riches available to us now. Paul writes in 2 Corinthians 3:18 that we "are being transformed into the same image from one degree of glory to another. For this comes from the Lord who is the Spirit." A Christian is a person with divine power to lead a heavenly life here on earth. Christians are not orphans but children and heirs (John 14:16–18), with a vast fortune held in trust from which we draw even now by faith, growing increasingly in the riches of grace and in the knowledge of God. Later in this chapter Paul prays that believers would know "the immeasurable greatness of [God's] power toward us who believe" (Eph. 1:19). Because of this power, despite our weakness and sin and overwhelming opposition, "we are more than conquerors through him who loved us" (Rom. 8:37). Christians have power through the Holy Spirit and are called to advance increasingly in godliness, especially as the Spirit applies God's Word, which is the special instrument of our growth and sanctification (John 17:17).

For this reason, Christians who think they cannot trust God in difficult situations, who think they can never overcome a particular temptation to sin, who think they cannot maintain their integrity in a dishonest workplace, who think they cannot love someone difficult in their lives, who think they cannot persevere through a trying situation, are wrong. They are failing to reckon with God's power available to us now by the Holy Spirit. We need to know about the Spirit—Paul says— who is a deposit on all that will be ours in heaven, including holiness and power for godliness, joy, peace, and love. Paul had high expectations for believers. Why? He says in Philippians 2:12–13, "Work out your own salvation with fear and trembling." He means that we should practically work our faith and obedience to God into every area of our lives. How can we do this? He adds, "for it is God who works in you, both to will and to work for his good pleasure."

Knowing this encourages us in the struggles of the present. But if we turn this around we gain an even greater encouragement regarding the future. For if the indwelling Spirit is merely a down payment on that which is yet to come, we can scarcely imagine how great is that which lies ahead. R. Kent Hughes rightly implores us:

> Imagine the sublimest, most treasured experiences of the Holy Spirit we have ever had and then realize they are only a foretaste, the tip of the tongue on the spoon, of what is to come. Remember the release in coming to Christ and knowing you were forgiven? Remember the time you followed the Spirit's leading and were wonderfully used? Remember the satisfaction of finding the fruits of the Spirit surprising you

with goodness where you once responded wickedly? Think of all this and then multiply it a millionfold. Here on earth we have experienced the first dollar of a million celestial dollars—the earnest. We have the dawning of knowledge, but then we will have the midday sun. "'No eye has seen, no ear has heard, no mind has conceived what God has prepared for those who love him'—but God has revealed it to us by his Spirit" (1 Cor. 2:9–10).[9]

If we have experience of these things then we know in kind what awaits us in heaven, though in magnitude we cannot begin to imagine such a weight of glory. So do you know something of these things? Do you know the release of sins forgiven? Do you know the satisfaction of useful service to God? Do you know the fruit of the Spirit and a power that has enabled you to turn away from sin? If you know nothing of these things, if it truly is all alien to your experience, then you cannot have the Spirit, and according to your own testimony you are not a Christian. You are in danger, the danger that you are like the rotten, rebellious children in Grisham's novel, vainly expecting an inheritance that has been given to others, namely, God's children who serve him in this world. While you live it up now you are piling up debts that will have to be paid, and soon the whole façade of your life will come crashing down. What you need is to go to Jesus, confess your sin and look to him, trust in him for your redemption, to be washed and renewed and restored to God, and to receive the promised Holy Spirit.

But if you do know about these things, if your heart leapt at the mention of the forgiveness of your sin, if you have knowledge of God through the light of his Word, then just imagine what it will be like when these things are multiplied by the infinite power and goodness of God! "How my heart yearns within me!" cried Job even in his sufferings, at the thought of what awaits him in the resurrection dawn (Job 19:27 NKJV). Thoughts of the same will cause our hearts to burn with anticipation, to sing with love for our Redeemer, to labor with zeal for the advance of his kingdom.

THE MOST VALUED PRAISE

We see, therefore, the significance of the Spirit's work in this present age of grace. His presence gives us assurance, for the down payment guarantees that all will be ours in due time. His lively working gives enjoyment, as we partake now in measure of blessings to come beyond our imagining. As a result, we ought to be all the more eager to live in this present age for the glory of our wonderful God. That is how Paul completes this verse, and this whole great hymn of praise to God. It is all "to the praise of his glory."

This is the third time Paul has used this expression. It first appeared with regard to God the Father in his work of ordaining our salvation: "He chose us in him before the foundation of the world, that we should be holy and blameless before him. In love he predestined us for adoption through Jesus Christ, according to the purpose of his will, to the praise of his glorious grace, with which he has blessed us in the Beloved" (Eph. 1:4–6). The work of the Father in eternity past, his glorious plan upheld even now and extending to eternity future, brings praise to the glory of his grace. Ephesians 1:12 similarly says our inclusion in Christ through faith is "for the praise of his glory." Now, in Ephesians 1:14, the giving of God's Spirit as the seal and deposit on our full redemption is also "to the praise of his glory."

Do you realize who is going to glorify God on the day of your final redemption? When the Bible describes the crowd of acclamation that will be praising God for his wondrous salvation of sinners like you and me, it includes an amazing host. It includes angels in the heavens. Revelation 7 depicts multitudes of the redeemed gathered all in white, with angels and the four living creatures standing around God's throne: "They fell on their faces before the throne and worshiped God, saying, 'Amen! Blessing and glory and wisdom and thanksgiving and honor and power and might be to our God forever and ever! Amen!'" (Rev. 7:11–12).

Do you realize that in the end the devil and the demons and all who followed them in hating God will have to acknowledge the glory of his grace in the matter of your salvation? Philippians 2:10–11 tells us, "At the name of Jesus every knee should bow, in heaven and on earth and under the earth, and every tongue confess that Jesus Christ is Lord, to the glory of God the Father."

And do you realize that the created realm will break forth in praise at the redemption of God's children? Romans 8:19 says, "The creation waits with eager longing for the revealing of the sons of God." Then will be its own deliverance from the fall, the regeneration of all things. Isaiah 55:12 tells us,

> The mountains and the hills before you
> > shall break forth into singing,
> > and all the trees of the field shall clap their hands.

And yet, with all that praise, from every corner of the universe, in heaven above and hell below, there is one voice of praise most precious to the heart of God. I mentioned that the Greek word for deposit is *arrabōn*, and it is an interesting fact that in the development of the Greek language that word came to be used for a wedding ring. That, too, is a way we should think about the indwelling of the Holy Spirit, as the ring God slips upon our finger, betrothing us to himself and pledging his devotion for the wedding that is yet to come.

As a minister, I do a lot of weddings, and I always enjoy the exchange of rings. I say to each party, "Have you a token to give of your fidelity to this covenant?" God likewise enters into covenant with us in Jesus Christ. He promises our full redemption in the glory yet to be revealed, and he gives to us the Spirit as a token of his fidelity. Putting the ring on the finger of his bride, the groom says, "I give you this ring as a symbol and pledge of my constant faith and abiding love." So is the presence of the Spirit in your life a symbol and pledge of God's constant faith and abiding love to you.

There is a wedding ahead for us, the bride of Christ entering into mutual possession with her Lord forever. This is how the Bible depicts us in the end. John writes, "I saw the holy city, new Jerusalem, coming down out of heaven from God, prepared as a bride adorned for her husband" (Rev. 21:2). If that is how the Bible portrays the consummation of all things, then let me ask you again, Whose praise do you think God will most delight to receive? There will be angels and archangels and four living creatures. There will be the stopped tongues of all God's foes—demonic and human—in hell. The whole creation will be in witness, extolling the redemption of God's cherished own. But when the doors of history open, when the bride finally strolls down the aisle, the eyes of the groom will rest only on her. For it is the adoration of the bride that most enthralls the heart of the groom.

What a privilege! What glory awaits us! And, that being the case, how much must God delight in our adoring praise now, as much he will then, so that the praise we give him now, for the glory of his grace in our redemption, is the most wonderful sound in all the vast creation. Let us, then, praise indeed our glorious God "who has blessed us in Christ with every spiritual blessing in the heavenly places," our loving husband and groom, our Savior and our Lord.

13

PAUL'S PRAYER FOR THE CHURCH

Ephesians 1:15–17

For this reason, because I have heard of your
faith in the Lord Jesus and your love toward all the saints,
I do not cease to give thanks for you, remembering you in my
prayers, that the God of our Lord Jesus Christ, the Father
of glory, may give you a spirit of wisdom and
of revelation in the knowledge of him.
—Ephesians 1:15–17

Prayer is the loftiest and most spiritual exercise of which we are capable as Christians. Prayer is having an audience with God, worshiping him directly, asking of him, and receiving spiritual blessings in his presence. It is no surprise, therefore, that prayer is difficult. That is why so many

Christians look on prayer as an irksome duty, a chore that we accept but only with reluctance. As a result, many of us think, "How much time must I spend in prayer?" rather than "How much time may I spend in prayer?"

Private prayer is a great blessing, but it is especially prayer together with other believers that lifts us up into heaven and gives us a heavenly-mindedness toward one another. For that reason it is important for Christians to pray for one another but also with one another. Along with membership in a solid church, regular Bible study, and private prayer, the importance of praying with other Christians should be stressed as part of the vital discipline of the Christian life.

It is especially wonderful to interact and pray with older Christians, those who have walked far longer with our Lord and thus have more extensive and intimate experience with Christ. One of the chief privileges I have had in my time in ministry is the benefit of personal access to eminent people of God, whose spirituality in prayer has had a most profound impact on me. I have profited from the preaching of others, from personal conversations and interactions. But above all, there is nothing like kneeling together with an older, godly Christian, coming together before the Lord to worship and seek blessings from on high.

Given all this, Christians should pay special attention to the prayers that are found in the Bible. In this chapter we begin to study a great prayer from the apostle Paul, a most eminent Christian whose spirituality flowed from a most singular relationship with and experience of Jesus Christ. In Paul's writings we have the prayers of one who is seasoned by decades of ground-breaking missionary labor, and better still, whose writings in Scripture possess the sanctity of biblical inspiration. The prayers we find in the Bible—in the Psalms, in the Old Testament histories and prophets, and in the New Testament epistles—are not merely the prayers of eminent believers but the prayers God inspired in them and revealed through them for our benefit. Apart from our Lord's direct teaching on prayer, there can hardly be more beneficial material for our prayer life than those from the mouths of prophets and apostles.

PAUL AS A MAN OF PRAYER

The apostle Paul is particularly noteworthy in this regard because of the great wealth of prayers we find in his letters. The Pauline epistles are laced with prayer, which probably reflects the intensity of Paul's spirituality, as well as the demands of his ministry. The first thing we learn about Paul after his conversion is the statement of Acts 9:11, where Ananias is told to find him in a certain house in Damascus, where "he is praying." The King James Version eloquently puts it, "Behold, he prayeth," which is not a bad beginning to anyone's spiritual biography. "It is as though," says Arthur Pink of Paul's attitude, "that struck the keynote of his subsequent life, that he would, to a special degree, be marked as a man of prayer."[1]

Paul's letters are filled with prayer no doubt because Paul's life was filled with prayer. If you follow his travels and log the intercessions he writes about in his letters, you get a glimpse at how far-flung were his concerns in prayer. He wrote to the Philippians, "I thank my God in all my remembrance of you, always in every prayer" (Phil. 1:3–4), language that is echoed in the verses of our passage. Paul's practice seems to have been to pray for whomever he is thinking. Whenever he heard a bit of news or recalled a person or a church he turned to the Lord on their behalf, thanking God for good news and interceding for their spiritual well-being. No wonder, then, that he represents himself as praying constantly. "I thank God," he wrote to Timothy, "as I remember you constantly in my prayers night and day" (2 Tim. 1:3). The man who exhorted us to pray without ceasing (1 Thess. 5:17) seems to have practiced what he preached. Though he was chained to Roman guards, Paul's ministry ranged far and wide in prayer.

We find a similar zeal with practically every Christian who has been greatly used by the Lord. Martin Luther often prayed two or three hours a day, and his great moments of faith were all preceded by long and fervent prayer. The Roman Catholic Church once sent an agent to spy out Luther's weaknesses, and the spy came back lamenting, "Who can overcome a man who prays like this?" John Calvin often rose at 4:00 A.M. for prayer. John Knox cried out to God, "Give me Scotland, or I die!" The same is true of leaders God used to bring revival to America. Jonathan Edwards spent whole days in prayer, seeking blessings for his people as well as power for his preaching. We find the same to be true of great men and women in the Bible. Moses, David, and Solomon are known for their prayers. Hezekiah, Daniel, Esther, Nehemiah, and Ezra all are shown in prayer before the defining moments of their careers. Of course, the greatest example is our Lord Jesus, who regularly went off alone for long periods of prayer.

These examples show the value of prayer to the Christian life. People will pay great sums of money and go to great effort to gain an audience with a famous or powerful person. But Christians have access to God himself. Surely this is our greatest dignity and privilege. We gain many benefits from prayer, temporal and eternal. But even apart from the benefit, we have in prayer an audience with the King of kings, the Lord of Hosts, with Almighty God! What is all the world in comparison with that! We have fellowship with God. "We read that Moses was upon the mountain forty days with God," writes Jeremiah Burroughs, "and when he came down his face so shone that the people were not able to bear it. . . . Converse much with God, be often with God, be near to Him and that will make you shine as lights in the midst of a crooked and perverse generation."[2] Indeed, those words spoken of Paul, "he is praying," are the best argument for any of us that our spiritual life is sound and prospering.

Paul was a man of prayer because he was a man of God. But his writings also stand out for their emphasis on prayer because of the demands of his leadership role in the fledgling church. Paul was the apostle to the Gentiles, a missionary who had ongoing relationships with a great many churches. He prayed for them as a shepherd cares for the sheep, just as pastors today are obliged to pray much for their congregation. Paul counted this as a duty, as well as a difficult burden. He wrote, "Apart from other things, there is the daily pressure on me of my anxiety for all the churches" (2 Cor. 11:28), and therefore he prayed.

Since so many of Paul's converts were former pagans, he may have felt a special need to write about his prayers so as to set a model for their spirituality. Furthermore, these early Christians often disappointed Paul, and prayer no doubt helped him to maintain a gracious spirit toward them. Dietrich Bonhoeffer emphasized this aspect of intercessory prayer in his account of life in the underground seminary he supervised in Nazi Germany. He wrote, "A Christian fellowship lives and exists by the intercession of its members for one another. . . . I can no longer condemn or hate a brother for whom I pray, no matter how much trouble he causes me. His face . . . is transformed in intercession into the countenance of a brother for whom Christ died, the face of a forgiven sinner."[3] Likewise, Paul's life of prayer no doubt fueled his patience and love for the often wayward churches he oversaw.

THE NECESSITY OF PRAYER

When we turn to this prayer in Ephesians 1, the first thing it shows is the necessity of prayer to any effective gospel ministry. Paul has just written, in Ephesians 1:3–14, some of the

173

most inspiring theological statements ever penned. And yet he obviously does not think it sufficient simply to set forth his teaching, unless he combines it with fervent prayers to God for his blessing. Pink explains, "The preacher's obligations are not fully discharged when he leaves the pulpit, for he needs to water the seed he has sown. . . . Paul mingled supplications with his instructions." Speaking of ministers, he adds, "It is our privilege and duty to retire to the secret place after we leave the pulpit and beg God to write His Word on the hearts of those who have listened to us, to prevent the enemy from snatching away the seed, to so bless our efforts that they may bear fruit to God's eternal praise."[4] Likewise, church members have a duty to pray for their ministers and for God's blessing on the preaching of his Word.

This points out a danger that arises from our high view of Scripture. We believe and proclaim the sufficiency of Scripture. We constantly trumpet that the Bible is all that we need for life and godliness, for the knowledge of God and for salvation. Yet that does not make the blessing of Scripture automatic. The doctrine of Scripture's sufficiency does not in any way lessen the need for prayer. God's Word is the singular instrument he has given for building up his church, but even it "works" only as God causes it to work. Salvation requires not merely the preaching of God's Word but also the ministry of the Holy Spirit to regenerate the sinful heart and enlighten the darkened mind, and for this we are to pray.

It is remembered at Tenth Presbyterian Church in Philadelphia that its long-time pastor, Donald Grey Barnhouse, could often be found in the sanctuary on Saturdays kneeling beside each pew, thinking about the people who often sat there and asking God to bless them with the following day's sermon. Every true minister knows what it is to feel his weakness and to labor in prayer for the supply of God's power. I often think of the example of Jesus when feeding the five thousand. Standing before the thousands with so little to give them, he prayed to the Father for supernatural blessing and then, having prayed, he was confident in distributing the few loaves and fishes that fed so great a multitude.

Here in Ephesians, we see the apostle setting down his pen after the elevated teaching of this chapter and beseeching God to enlighten his readers' hearts that they might come to know him. If that kind of prayer was necessary to Paul, it surely is necessary for us.

THANKS FOR FAITH AND LOVE

In Ephesians 1:15 Paul explains his reason for praying. "For this reason," he begins, pointing back to the whole of what he had taught in Ephesians 1:3–14. The emphasis of that teaching was on God's sovereignty in salvation. Many people consider this to be a disincentive to prayer, but it is the reason Paul prays. Paul is reflecting on the faith and love of the Ephesian Christians, and it is because God is sovereign in salvation that he prays to give God thanks for them. Paul does not credit the Christians for their faith and love, but God. D. A. Carson explains, "Apart from God's powerful transforming work, these people would never have been converted. Without God, they would never have begun to display the trust, faithfulness, and love now richly displayed in their lives. Therefore whatever Christian virtues characterize them become the occasion for heartfelt praise to God."[5]

If God's sovereignty is the reason Paul prays with thanksgiving, the occasion of his prayer is learning of the Ephesians' faith and love. "For this reason," he explains, "because I have heard of your faith in the Lord Jesus and your love toward all the saints, I do not cease to give thanks for you, remembering you in my prayers" (Eph. 1:15–16).

Notice what excites Paul when it comes to the church. I

don't think it is an exaggeration to say that what excites many in the church today is far different from what excited Paul. We are thrilled to see worldly measures of success, when attendance is up, when the church acquires money and worldly power. These things are not bad in themselves, but far more important is what Paul prays for—"faith in the Lord Jesus and love toward all the saints." James Montgomery Boice commented:

> Faith really is the essential thing, not numbers or programs, not budgets or buildings. It is by faith that we "demolish arguments and every pretension that sets itself up against the knowledge of God, and we take captive every thought to make it obedient to Christ." (2 Cor. 10:5). The apostle John said, "This is the victory that has overcome the world, even our faith" (1 John 5:4).[6]

Without faith and love, the church fails in its mission, however many people, however much money or power we acquire. But with faith and love, the church is often vibrant and effective in spiritual terms, even when there are numerically few of us, when we are poor and downcast in the world. These are the things Paul constantly looked for in his churches, prayed for, and thanked God to see.

If we compare Paul's prayers to different churches we will see just how consistent he was in this regard. He wrote to the Colossians, "We always thank God, the Father of our Lord Jesus Christ, when we pray for you, since we heard of your faith in Christ Jesus and of the love that you have for all the saints" (Col. 1:3–4). To Philemon he wrote, "I thank my God always when I remember you in my prayers, because I hear of your love and of the faith that you have toward the Lord Jesus and all the saints" (Philem. 4–5). In 2 Thessalonians, he prays, "We ought always to give thanks to God for you, brothers, as is right, because your faith is growing abundantly, and the love of every one of you for one another is increasing" (2 Thess. 1:3). There is a lesson for us here in the priorities of Paul's prayers. If faith is what Paul values and prays for, and if, as Paul says in Romans 10:17, "faith comes from hearing," then we ought to make the proclamation of the gospel our great priority, along with loving community in the family of the church.

To rightly understand Paul, we must define what it means to have faith in the Lord. We hear a lot today about faith in God in a general sort of way. But Paul would not be thankful that people maintained a bare theism or a merely religious outlook on life, until they trusted the crucified and risen Lord Jesus for their salvation. Many people believe in the idea of God and may be fine moral people, and yet they are not Christians. They are not saved; they still abide under the wrath of God. It is not enough to look on Jesus as a great moral figure or even as a teacher that we should emulate. We must look to him as the Son of God, as the Savior of sinners through the blood of his cross, and as the resurrected and living Lord, to be saved by the faith for which Paul gives thanks. Jesus said, "No one comes to the Father except through me" (John 14:6). "God put [him] forward as a propitiation," Paul writes in Romans 3:25, "by his blood, to be received by faith." The Philippian jailer asked Paul, "What must I do to be saved?" It is in this sense, in view of his cross and empty tomb, that Paul replied, "Believe in the Lord Jesus, and you will be saved" (Acts 16:30–31).

Just as striking in Paul's prayers is the emphasis he places on love, especially the saints' love for other believers. Again, Paul is consistent in mentioning love along with faith. The clear implication is that without love our faith cannot be considered genuine and true. Our faith is validated not merely by doctrinal correctness but by our love for others, especially other believers. Here is a proof for which the devil has no an-

177

swer, the love of Christians one for another, our readiness to give for brothers and sisters, the tears of one saint for the trials of another, the palpable joy in the Lord that marks true Christian fellowship. John writes, "Beloved, if God so loved us, we also ought to love one another. No one has ever seen God; if we love one another, God abides in us and his love is perfected in us" (1 John 4:11–12).

Christianity must always be defined in terms of truth and life. This is why Paul's letters are so regularly divided into two sections: one lays out doctrine, and the other applies the doctrine in terms of our lives. Ephesians is a classic example of this pattern, the first three and a half chapters presenting doctrine and the last two and half chapters applying it practically. Christianity, Paul says, consists of faith and of love. Therefore, he says in Galatians 5:6 that what really matters is "faith working through love."

LOVE AS THE TEST AND WITNESS OF FAITH

The requirement to love one another often turns out to be quite a challenge, and our failure in this regard often mars the witness of the church. William Edgar, writing on this topic, recalls the situation of the small and struggling Protestant church in France. During the twentieth century this Christian body possessed two world-class theologians, both of whom were experts on John Calvin. The two were bitter enemies, despite their shared theology and loyalty to the same church. Most of their differences were over technical matters: for instance, had Calvin read the writings of Copernicus before writing his commentary on Genesis? Over such issues the two men waged relentless conflict all the way to the grave. Edgar notes that the church they loved "remains small and ineffective to this day, and it cries out for solid teachers who can build up rather than destroy."[7] As another example, Edgar notes two seminary professors who waged a heated battle in prominent journals. After many years a student asked one of them why things had become so bitter. The professor commented that the two of them had never sat down to talk about their differences, which the student found surprising since the professors taught at the same seminary.

Why is love so hard? The answer is our sin. But it is our union with Christ through faith that makes love possible for sinners and obligatory for Christians. The basis of our love is our shared allegiance to Christ, but even more important is the shared Holy Spirit who lives within us. The Puritan Richard Sibbes wrote, "As we are knit to Christ by faith, so we must be knit to the communion of saints by love."[8]

Anyone who underestimates the challenge of love within the church probably has not been a Christian very long. It is not easy to love people who are different even when they are Christians, and who in many cases have sinned against you and you against them. Love among Christians therefore requires that we be ready to repent of our own sins, that we be eager to forgive those who have sinned against us, and that we turn to the Lord in fresh faith and obedience, seeking his aid through the Holy Spirit. Repentance, forgiveness, and new obedience—all these are fruits of our faith that allow us to love.

The stakes could not be higher, for at stake is the spiritual health of the church as well as its witness before the world. Jesus said, "As I have loved you, you also are to love one another. By this all people will know that you are my disciples, if you have love for one another" (John 13:34–35). Francis Schaeffer explained:

> Without true Christians loving one another, Christ says the world cannot be expected to listen, even when we give proper answers. . . . After we have done our best to communicate to a lost world, still we must never for-

get that the final apologetic which Jesus gives is the observable love of true Christians for true Christians. . . . if the world does not see this, it will not believe that Christ was sent by the Father.[9]

No wonder Paul thanked God for the faith and love of the Ephesians! Whenever we see Christians living together in truth and in love, it is a sure sign that the Holy Spirit is at work through faith in Jesus Christ. Truth without love is not Christian truth; love without truth is not Christian love. Either without the other falsely represents God before the world. It is only with truth and love held together, as the Holy Spirit works through our faith in Christ, that the true God of the Bible is revealed to the eyes of the watching world.

THE SECRET OF PRAYER

Paul's great desire was not only that the Ephesians should reveal God to the world but also that they themselves should come to know him better. This is the primary request that he adds to the thanksgiving of this prayer, "That the God of our Lord Jesus Christ, the Father of glory, may give you a spirit of wisdom and of revelation in the knowledge of him" (Eph. 1:17).

The next chapter will focus on knowing God, but we should observe in closing that it is primarily through the Bible that God's people come to know him, and it is through prayer that we come to rightly understand the Bible. Paul sets the example in this chapter, joining his teaching to fervent prayer. Boice writes, "If we are to know God, we must spend time with him in Bible study, prayer, and meditation. You cannot get to know a person without spending time with him or her. No more can you get to know God without spending time with him."[10]

The famous evangelist Harry Ironside illustrates this with an incident from early in his ministry. He went to visit a godly old man who was soon to die. While listening to the man talk of God, he was amazed at the man's astonishing knowledge of Scripture and grasp of truth. Before long, tears were streaming down Ironside's cheeks, and he asked, "Where did you get these things? Can you tell me where I can find a book that will open them up to me? Did you get them in a seminary or college?" The old man replied:

> My dear young man, I learned these things on my knees on the mud floor of a little sod cottage in the north of Ireland. There with my Bible open before me, I used to kneel for hours at a time and ask the Spirit of God to reveal Christ to my soul and to open the Word to my heart, and he taught me more on my knees on that mud floor than I ever could have learned in all the seminaries or colleges in the world.[11]

Prayer and the Word. There is the secret to knowing God, to growing in faith and learning to love other Christians. It is people who sit at Jesus' feet, who spend time with God in prayer and through the Word, who thereby come to know him better and then reveal him to the eyes of the world.

14

KNOWING GOD

Ephesians 1:17

*That the God of our Lord Jesus Christ,
the Father of glory, may give you a spirit of wisdom and of
revelation in the knowledge of him.*
—Ephesians 1:17

Imagine yourself receiving a note from a trusted Christian mentor or advisor—perhaps a parent or former teacher—someone who knows you and loves you. The note tells you that the person has been praying for you and even informs you of the content of those prayers. Perhaps the note speaks of a prayer for you to have patience. This would suggest that in his or her view this is something you lack or otherwise need. Perhaps the prayers were for contentment or zeal for the Lord's work. Those prayers would suggest that you may suffer from discontentedness or laziness.

In Ephesians 1:17 we have the apostle Paul writing to tell the Ephesian Christians what he has been praying for them. This was a church Paul was close to, having planted it and tended its growth for two years. He knew them and loved them. However, we observed that this letter was likely sent as a circular treatise, not only to the church in Ephesus but also to those in the area surrounding. This is therefore a general letter, written not only for particular errors or needs but for the general edification of the church.

Paul has heard about their faith and love, as he tells us in Ephesians 1:15, and he has been thanking God and praying for them. In Ephesians1:17 we have Paul's primary request, which suggests his sense of their greatest need: He prays "that the God of our Lord Jesus Christ, the Father of glory, may give you a spirit of wisdom and of revelation in the knowledge of him."

THE PRIORITY OF KNOWING GOD

If we were to make a list of the pressing needs of the church today it would not take much thought to add quite a few items. We live in a godless, unbelieving culture, so we have a great need for evangelism and apologetics. Furthermore, there is gross ignorance within the church, so we need sound Bible preaching and teaching. Because of the mounting worldliness evident in the church, we need more holiness. Furthermore, as pagan ideals impact the government and culture, we need to get involved in civic life. Such things require money, so we need financial resources. All of these needs are real, and all would have been needed in Paul's day much as in our own.

But when Paul relates his primary desire for the church, the Christians' greatest need, he turns to none of these. He prays that our God and Father would send the Spirit of wisdom and revelation, for "the knowledge of him," or as the New International Version puts it, "so that you may know him better." What does Paul most desire? That they may know God and know him increasingly.

The importance of this matter is highlighted when we realize that this is the very thing our Lord Jesus prayed for in John 17 on the night of his arrest. There, Jesus gave a great definition of salvation, praying to the Father, "And this is eternal life, that they know you the only true God, and Jesus Christ whom you have sent" (John 17:3). Eternal life is knowing God, and it is for this that Paul chiefly prays. This is the heart and the fulfillment of God's covenant purpose, as stated in Jeremiah's new covenant promise: "I will be their God, and they shall be my people. And no longer shall each one teach his neighbor and each his brother, saying, 'Know the LORD,' for they shall all know me, from the least of them to the greatest, declares the LORD" (Jer. 31:33–34). Knowing God is always the greatest need of the church, for, as John Calvin writes, "The final goal of the blessed life rests in the knowledge of God."[1]

In his study of Paul's prayers, New Testament scholar D. A. Carson singles out the knowledge of God as "the urgent need of the church." Speaking of the other things I have listed, he writes:

> Clearly all of these things are important. I would not want anything I have said to be taken as disparagement of evangelism and worship, a diminishing of the importance of purity and integrity, a carelessness about disciplined Bible study. But there is a sense in which these urgent needs are merely symptomatic of a far more serious lack. The one thing we most urgently need in Western Christendom is a deeper knowledge of God. We need to know God better.

We need, he says, to be turned away from our felt needs, away from happiness and fulfillment as we understand them temporally, and turned toward the glories and excellences of God. "We think rather little of what he is like," Carson observes, "what he expects of us, what he seeks in us. We are not captured by his holiness and his love; his thoughts and words capture too little of our imagination, too little of our discourse, too few of our priorities."[2] The great need of the church today, therefore, as of the church in the apostle's time, is knowledge of God.

When Paul writes about knowing God, he speaks of personal, experiential knowledge. But this knowledge of God starts with knowing about God. A doctrinal knowledge of God is essential. For this reason, few studies are more profitable than the attributes of God. On God's character, his unchanging attributes, we utterly depend for our salvation; knowing about God is essential to a relationship with God.

When we speak of God's attributes, we mean aspects of his character, descriptions of what God is like as taught by the Bible. They are not things God has or possesses, but ways that God *is*. They are affirmations and denials regarding his being and character that lead us into a true knowledge of him. God is holy, good, just, and true—those are all affirmations made in the Scripture. In other respects, God can only be described negatively: he is infinite—that is, he cannot be contained or exhausted; he is immutable—he cannot change; he is immense—he cannot be measured.

As you read the Bible you should be thinking about what the text is teaching you about God. In the creation account we learn of God's eternal nature, his wisdom, his power, and especially his glory. "The heavens declare the glory of God," David sings (Ps. 19:1). Noah's flood, the destruction of Sodom and Gomorrah, and other judgments reveal to us that God is holy and just. In the exodus we learn that God is faithful and good but also mighty to save. Through all these and other accounts God shows us what he is like, knowledge that is essential to our faith.

186

I want to give three reasons why we should study God in his person and his works. The first is the excellence of the subject matter. Charles Spurgeon commented:

> There is something exceedingly improving to the mind in a contemplation of the Divinity. It is a subject so vast, that all our thoughts are lost in its immensity; so deep, that our pride is drowned in its infinity. . . . But while the subject humbles the mind, it also expands it. Nothing will so enlarge the intellect, nothing so magnify the whole soul of man, as a devout, earnest, continuing investigation of the great subject of the Deity.[3]

It is through the knowledge of God that we come truly to know ourselves and then attain to that which we were created to be.

Second, by studying and coming to know God we find a ready comfort for our fears and are made bold for obedience. I think this is what makes the attributes of God such an important study for children. My daughter was able to overcome her fear of separation as a little child because of what she learned about God in the children's catechism. One question she learned was, "Can you see God?" The answer meant a lot to her: "No, I cannot see God, but he can always see me." Knowing that gave her confidence when separated from her parents.

Christians are likewise comforted in trials to know that God is wise in all things, that he is almighty, that he is holy and good and loving. Those things being true, we see why Romans 8:28 can tell us, "For those who love God all things work together for good, for those who are called according to his purpose." Knowing who and what God is, Paul reasons, "If God is for us, who can be against us?" (Rom. 8:31). Because of who he is, nothing in all creation "will be able to separate us from the love of God in Christ Jesus our Lord" (Rom. 8:39).

The knowledge of God not only comforts us but also emboldens us for obedience. In Isaiah 6, the prophet saw a vision of the Lord in all his holy majesty. Isaiah 7 goes on to show how the prophet boldly confronted the king of Judah when he entered into idolatrous alliances. Where did Isaiah get the boldness of Isaiah 7? It came from the knowledge of God that he discovered in the vision of Isaiah 6.

We should study God because of the elevating influence of the subject matter and to give us the comfort and boldness we so greatly need.

The third reason is that our beliefs regarding God profoundly shape our understanding of the salvation he gives. How we relate to God, what expectations we have of the Christian life, and what we hope for in the future all depend on the kind of God he is. Defective views of God always exert a corrupting influence on our views of salvation.

One important example today is what is called open theism. This is a heresy that denies that God exhaustively knows the future. God is, according to proponents of this view, deficient in his understanding and as such he occasionally makes mistakes and is overcome by events. While God surely is resourceful, they say, he is able neither to predict future events nor to control them with certainty. This teaching denies God's foreknowledge and sovereignty and ultimately compromises such attributes as God's infinity and wisdom and immutability. So opposed is this view to the picture of God in the Bible that you may be surprised to learn that one large evangelical denomination has accepted it and a number of prominent evangelical institutions—including publishing houses and leading magazines—have actively propagated this false teaching.

Is this harmless speculation or is there real danger? I think the assessment Bruce Ware gives in his critique of open theism is correct. He asks, "Can our hope in God to fulfill his promises be founded without mental reservation or qualification? Can a believer know that God will triumph in the future just as he promised he will?"[4] The answers depend on the kind of God he is. Ware is right when he says the openness heresy undermines our confidence, hope, and reliance on the Lord. He explains:

> To the extent that the openness model of God penetrates our churches, we can anticipate a greatly lessened confidence in God and a much greater temptation to trust in our own insights and abilities. We can anticipate weakened prayer lives and more confidence in our own accomplishments. God will be viewed increasingly as a pathetic sort of figure, possessing good motives but terribly faulty in his attempts to steer the direction of our lives and of human history.[5]

How can such a terrible denial of important attributes of God have spread so far through the so-called Bible-believing world? The only explanation is that we have lost sight of God. We have lost interest in him and forgotten him. This is always how the problems began in Old Testament Israel. Judges 2:10, for instance, tells us, "There arose another generation after them who did not know the LORD." If we want to avoid damaging errors today, to preserve the vigor of the Christian faith for future generations, to know the blessings God offers, and to have our names added to the roster of the faithful, then we must follow the desire of Paul's prayer and make it our business to know God.

GOD REVEALED THROUGH JESUS CHRIST

All of that falls under the heading of our first point, the priority of knowing God. The second point made by this verse is that God is most singularly known and revealed through his

Son Jesus Christ. This is something Jesus boldly insisted. Matthew 11:27 is one of many statements to this effect: Jesus said, "No one knows the Son except the Father, and no one knows the Father except the Son and anyone to whom the Son chooses to reveal him." That explains why, in praying that we would know God, Paul refers to him as "the God of our Lord Jesus Christ, the Father of glory."

God's highest and best revelation of himself to humankind is through his Son Jesus Christ. In 1 Timothy 6:16, Paul tells us that God lives in "unapproachable light." God is himself, as a spirit, invisible. Therefore he reveals himself not by taking things off but by putting them on. To Moses he showed himself as a burning bush. To Israel he came as a pillar of fire and smoke. But ultimately, he revealed himself by taking on human form, entering into our world and walking among us. God's highest revelation of himself to us is through his Son, the man Jesus Christ. Therefore Paul writes in 2 Corinthians 4:6 that God shined his light in our hearts "to give the light of the knowledge of the glory of God in the face of Jesus Christ." Jesus is, says Hebrews 1:3, "the radiance of the glory of God and the exact imprint of his nature." God reveals himself to us through the person and work of Jesus Christ, who is "the image of the invisible God" (Col. 1:15).

This is why Paul writes the way he does in Ephesians 1:17. The God he prays that we will know is "the God of our Lord Jesus Christ, the Father of glory," who is revealed to us through the Son. And yet we are not meant merely to know about the true God by means of Jesus. More than that, it is through the ministry of God's Son, in union with Jesus Christ through faith, that we come into a personal and loving relationship with the true God. Jesus has come not merely that we might know about God more accurately, but that we should be reconciled to him through Christ's blood and become God's children, knowing him as our heavenly Father.

Jesus made this point to Mary Magdalene when she recognized him after his resurrection. Jesus told her to inform the disciples that he had risen and then said, "I am ascending to my Father and your Father, to my God and your God" (John 20:17). His point was that having accomplished his work on earth as our Savior, he now would return to heaven in order to complete our reconciliation. The God he had known in intimacy as the Son would now be a Father to us. "I will be their God and they will be my people," God so often promised in Scripture, and now in Christ all that is realized.

Having revealed himself through Jesus Christ, God invites you to know him in a personal way, to enter into his love as his beloved child, coming to God through Christ's saving work. The apostle John wrote of Jesus, "To all who did receive him, who believed in his name, he gave the right to become children of God" (John 1:12).

In Ephesians 3, Paul prays in a manner very similar to the prayer here in Ephesians 1. There, he reminds us that it is especially through the cross that God is revealed to sinful humankind and invites us to come to him. "I pray," Paul writes, "that you . . . may have strength to comprehend with all the saints what is the breadth and length and height and depth, and to know the love of Christ that surpasses knowledge, that you may be filled with all the fullness of God" (Eph. 3:17–19). That is ultimately what Paul means by knowing God through Jesus Christ: being filled with the abundant and eternal life God gives to sinners who are reconciled through the work of his Son.

GOD KNOWN THROUGH THE MINISTRY OF THE HOLY SPIRIT

In the great doxology that began the Book of Ephesians, we noted the trinitarian framework with which Paul presented the blessings of salvation. Now that we turn to the matter of knowing God, it is no surprise that Paul keeps this emphasis. To that end, he now directs us to the Holy Spirit. He has noted the priority of knowing God, knowledge of whom comes through the Son. He now prays that God "may give you a spirit of wisdom and of revelation." Our third point, therefore, is that God is known through the ministry of the Holy Spirit.

We speak of the process of revelation in terms of God's sending the Spirit to inspire the biblical authors. The Bible is his revealed Word because, as Peter puts it, "men spoke from God as they were carried along by the Holy Spirit" (2 Peter 1:21). Yet the revelation process does not cease with the inspiring of Scripture. God also sends the Spirit to us so that we are given spiritual understanding of what the Bible says. This is referred to as the Spirit's illuminating work. He reveals to us not things left out of the Scripture, not mystic clues hidden in the Scripture, but rather the plain truths he inspired in the Bible, which without his illumination would remain dark to our fallen minds.

There is debate about whether Paul is referring in this verse to God's Spirit—with a capital S, as the New International Version does—or merely to our human spirits—with a small s, as the English Standard Version and New King James Version do. Is he praying for God to send the Holy Spirit or merely to empower our spirituality? On the basis of Paul's trinitarian approach, and because of his typical usage elsewhere, I think we rightly see this as a reference to the Holy Spirit. But even in the latter case, Paul implies the need for God's Spirit to work within us. F. F. Bruce explains, "A 'spirit of wisdom and revelation' can be imparted only through him who is the personal Spirit of wisdom and revelation. . . . Only as God reveals by his Spirit can his people understand by that same Spirit."[6]

The passage where Paul most clearly explains the necessity of the Holy Spirit's illuminating work is 1 Corinthians 2.

Paul tells us there that because of our sinful, spiritually dead natures, it is necessary for the Spirit to work within us so that we comprehend and receive what God has said. Paul explains, "The natural person does not accept the things of the Spirit of God, for they are folly to him, and he is not able to understand them because they are spiritually discerned" (1 Cor. 2:14). The reason sinful people do not accept God's Word, he says, is that they cannot, they are not able, being spiritually dead and blind. Augustine explained, "Just as the sun is not seen by the blind, though they are clothed as it were with its rays, so is the light of truth not understood by the darkness of folly."[7] This is what Jesus said to Nicodemus: "Unless one is born again he cannot see the kingdom of God" (John 3:3). Apart from the enlivening, eye-opening work of God's Spirit, sinners not only cannot enter God's kingdom but also cannot even see it in the light of God's Word.

No wonder, then, that Paul prays for God to send the Spirit to give us wisdom and revelation. These two terms speak of the ability not merely to receive God's Word but also to digest it, so that we are made, as Paul says to Timothy, "wise for salvation through faith in Christ Jesus" (2 Tim. 3:15). Evidence of this work of the Spirit is seen in the faith and love Paul commends in the Ephesians. But he prays, as we should, for more of this work so that we might know God better.

KNOWING GOD THROUGH THE WORD AND PRAYER

Putting this all together, this is Paul's prayer: that his readers would know God—in terms of understanding and of a relationship—as Jesus Christ reveals him and brings us to the Father in faith, and as the Holy Spirit works in our hearts with his regenerating and illuminating work. That is an excellent prayer—one we ought to pray for ourselves and for others.

But, as always, the Christian life consists of more than asking God for things in prayer. Our prayers imply a final point, which is a question: What are we to do to pursue the knowledge of God?

The answer, I think, is found in Paul's example. He wants his readers to know God, so he has written them with his teaching. As Paul will insist later in this letter (Eph. 3:2–5), he writes not as a private person but as God's appointed ambassador, giving them authorized teaching on God's behalf. If we want to know God, then we must become students of this and other books in the Bible. Jesus once prayed for us, saying, "Sanctify them in the truth; your word is truth" (John 17:17). Search through the Bible to find those who knew God and boldly did his will. You will find that they were people of God's Word, giving themselves to its study and learning in it to know and serve God. Search the annals of church history, and you will find the same. We, too, must be people of God's book.

Do you want to know God? Do you want to experience his presence in your life? Do you want to receive the fullness of his grace as you walk through this life with him? Then give yourself to his Word, the Bible, and he will meet with you there and show you his glory.

Paul also shows us that if we want to know God we must be people of prayer. Isn't that the combination we find in this great chapter—Scripture and prayer together? In prayer we ask for the Spirit's illuminating work so that we will profit from the Bible, and we come into communion with the Father through the access gained by the Son.

To some people this seems tedious and mundane. Ours is a mystical age in the church, and people do not want to have to study the Bible and think, or to order their lives to make room for prayer. They want to know God through some foolproof method that fits into their busy lives. Instead of walking step by step up the slopes of Mount Zion, they want to be flown directly to the top in a helicopter! I have noticed, in this re-

gard, that many top-selling Christian books today tell ministers to stop laboring on their sermons, to cease trying painstak-
ingly to teach the Bible. Instead, they are to act impulsively,
this being supposedly more spiritual. They are to aim for the
emotions rather than the mind, to seek to produce ecstatic,
nonrational experiences instead of the more tedious work of
knowing God as he reveals himself in the Bible.

In reading such material I am reminded of the experience of the prophet Elijah, who also wanted to hear from God,
to be encouraged by a direct encounter with the divine. Elijah went up Mount Horeb seeking God, and there he learned
a lesson we need to learn as well. Setting the prophet out on
the mountain, God told Elijah to await his coming.

> And a great and strong wind tore the mountains and
> broke in pieces the rocks before the LORD, but the
> LORD was not in the wind. And after the wind an earth-
> quake, but the LORD was not in the earthquake. And
> after the earthquake a fire, but the LORD was not in
> the fire. And after the fire the sound of a low whisper.
> (1 Kings 19:11–12)

It was in the whisper that God spoke to his prophet. Likewise, it is not in the experience of spiritual highs that we should
seek the knowledge of God. Rather, it is as we sit quietly with
the Bible on our laps, as we draw apart in prayer, as we come
to church and sit before faithful preaching—it is in this way
that we come to know God. We come to know him step by step
as we walk through our lives as people of his Book, as people
of prayer, looking to him in faith. We trust him in our need,
we obey him in temptation, we serve him in the world, we look
to him with tear-filled eyes in times of sorrow, we laugh with
thanks in times of joy. And through his Word and in prayer we
come to know him better, as we trust and obey, through faith

in Jesus Christ and by the power of the Holy Spirit that he sends. As the hymnist put it, this is how we come to know God:

> When we walk with the Lord
> In the light of his Word,
> What a glory he sheds on our way!
> While we do his good will,
> He abides with us still,
> And with all who will trust and obey.[8]

15

THE THREE "WHATS"

Ephesians 1:18–20

Having the eyes of your hearts enlightened, that
you may know what is the hope to which he has called you,
what are the riches of his glorious inheritance in the saints,
and what is the immeasurable greatness of his power toward
us who believe, according to the working of his great might
that he worked in Christ when he raised him from the dead
and seated him at his right hand in the heavenly places.
—Ephesians 1:18–19

When Nebuchadnezzar had conquered Jerusalem, he brought Judah's king, Zedekiah, to his capital city of Babylon. There in the imperial center, Zedekiah might console himself on the sights of the world's greatest city. He might look upon grand halls and palaces, the hanging garden that was a wonder of the world, the vast walls in formidable sentinel. But Zedekiah saw none of these things, for before his journey to Babylon his eyes had been put out. Instead of beholding beauty and wealth and glory, all of which were there before him, he lived in grim and dreary darkness.

In this great prayer which concludes Ephesians 1, the apostle Paul is determined that this should not be the case with his Christian readers. He prays that "the eyes of your hearts [may be] enlightened." He prays that we might see what is truly before us, yet which because of our spiritual blindness we utterly fail to perceive apart from the Spirit's enlightening work. The Bible says the natural man, because of the sinful condition of his heart and mind, is blind to the glories and beauties of God. Jesus said, "Unless one is born again he cannot see the kingdom of God" (John 3:3). Paul is praying here for believers, those who have been born again by the Spirit through the Word to a saving faith in Jesus Christ. Yet we, too, require the ongoing illumination of God's Spirit, whom Paul has described in the prior verse as "the Spirit of wisdom and revelation" (NIV).

In his great allegory, *Pilgrim's Progress,* John Bunyan tells of his hero, Christian, who after climbing the Hill of Difficulty stayed for a rest at the Castle Beautiful. There, Christian received instruction as well as a shield and a sword, and soon he was ready to resume his sojourn to the Celestial City. But before he went, the castle owners took him up on a hill to gaze ahead to where his destination could just be seen. There in the Delectable Mountains was the city he sought, and the sight of it emboldened him for the troubles yet ahead.

Paul wants the same for us, that eyes would be opened in our hearts, so that we might gain a spiritual apprehension of the blessings that are ours in Christ. This, he knows, will embolden us for the trials of our pilgrimage toward heaven. Three things particularly are on his mind, the knowledge of which he says constitutes an enlightened life, a life lived in the light of God's favor even in a dark and dangerous world. These are expressed in terms of three *whats* that we should know, namely, "what is the hope to which he has called you, what are the riches of his glorious inheritance in the saints, and what is the immeasurable greatness of his power toward us who believe."

THE HOPE TO WHICH HE HAS CALLED YOU

First, Paul prays that we may know what is "the hope to which he has called you," or more literally, what is "the hope of his calling." For most people the word *hope* means little more than a feeble optimism or wishful thinking. But the hope that Paul mentions in his letters is a mighty certainty of things looked for though not yet experienced. What makes Christian hope so strong is our confidence in God, who calls us to follow and promises us great blessing.

When we think of God's calling, we think of Abraham, who was called by God while living in Ur of the Chaldees. Abraham had done nothing to earn God's favor, and there is no evidence that he was seeking God in any way. Joshua 24:2 tells us that, like his father, Abraham worshiped other gods. But God came to him and called him out of the darkness of sin and condemnation to walk before him in faith. God gave him great promises. He said, "Fear not, Abram, I am your shield; your reward shall be very great" (Gen. 15:1).

This is how anyone is saved, that God comes to us in our sin, calling us to be separated out from the world, no longer to live as we have, and looking to God with hope for what he promises in the gospel. Christ calls generally throughout the world; his general call brings an offer of salvation to all who hear. The problem is, as Jesus so often lamented, that having ears they yet fail to hear. So God then calls some in particular, whom he has sovereignly ordained for eternal life. To them goes the effectual call, that which carries with it the power of God to believe the gospel, which presses it upon our hearts and causes us to follow. This is how Jesus gathered his twelve disciples. He said to them, "You did not choose me, but I chose you and appointed you that you should go and bear fruit and that your fruit should abide" (John 15:16). In this same sense "the called" are Christians, and Christians are "the called."

Abraham's hope arose from his calling. What was he hoping for but a new homeland and that from him would come a new people. "In hope he believed against hope," Paul writes. "He grew strong in his faith as he gave glory to God fully convinced that God was able to do what he had promised" (Rom. 4:18–21).

What is the hope to which God has called us? First, we think of the things we have already received. Paul wrote of them earlier in the chapter: election to holiness, adoption into the rights and rank of children of God. We have redemption through Christ's blood, the forgiveness of sins, and entrance into the mystery of God's saving plan. What a great hope is this! Like Abraham, we are called to a new world in Christ, to membership in God's family, and we look forward with hope to an ever increasing grasp of these privileges.

To these we add the hope of all we will need to sustain us in the faith. Charles Spurgeon writes eloquently of the Christian's hope:

> First, he hopes and believes that he shall be under divine protection for ever and ever, that he shall be the object of divine love time out of mind, and when time shall be no more. . . . He expects a stormy voyage, but because Christ is at the helm he hopes to come to the fair havens at the last. He expects to be tempted, but he hopes to be upheld. He expects to be slandered, but he hopes to be cleared. He expects to be tried, but

he hopes to triumph. Sustained by this hope he dreads
no labors and fears no difficulties.[1]

The Christian thus finds hope all through the Bible. We
turn to Psalm 23 and learn to hope to have the Lord as our
shepherd. We hope not to want, to find green pastures and
quiet waters, we hope for the restoration of our souls. We hope
that in the valley of the shadow of death he will be with us, that
goodness and mercy will follow us all the days of our lives until we dwell in the house of the Lord forever.

Paul wants us to know what is the hope of our calling. So
let me ask you, What is your hope? Are you hoping just to get
along, to stay out of trouble, to have a little fun along the way?
Are you hoping to store up a rampart of money and power, fame
and achievement, that these will hold out life's storms and bring
you the fullness you desire? Are you hoping in your ability, in the
success of the corporation or the country, in your degrees or
your connections? All of those things, though valuable perhaps
in some sense, will fail to sustain you or to fulfill the longings of
your soul. If it does not happen earlier, it is death that finally
brushes aside every false support, every vain hope in this world.

But if you know what is the hope of the Christian's calling, then you have a hope that can stand up against life and
death. Psalm 27:1 says:

> The LORD is my light and my salvation;
>   whom shall I fear?
> The LORD is the stronghold of my life;
>   of whom shall I be afraid?

Isaiah therefore says:

> Those who hope in the LORD
>   will renew their strength.

They will soar on wings like eagles;
> they will run and not grow weary,
> they will walk and not be faint. (Isa. 40:31 NIV)

What a difference it makes to ground our hope on God's calling, rather than a decision we made or a resolve we took up. If our salvation originates from something in us, it will have to be sustained by something in us. But if our hope arises from the calling of God, from his purpose and promise and power, then that is a sure hope in which we may trust and rejoice even in times of trial.

THE RICHES OF HIS GLORIOUS INHERITANCE

Second, Paul wants to enlighten us as to "what are the riches of his glorious inheritance in the saints." There is debate as to the meaning of this statement. One view is that Paul refers to the riches that God has in his inheritance in the saints. The roster of advocates of this view is impressive, including P. T. O'Brien, D. A. Carson, F. F. Bruce, Andrew Lincoln, and Charles Spurgeon. In this case Paul is referring to the riches of glory that God acquires for himself through our salvation. The Old Testament often spoke in this way. Psalm 33:12 says, "Blessed is the nation whose God is the LORD, the people whom he has chosen as his heritage!" God has invested in us his love and wisdom, his workmanship and care, and especially the precious blood of his Son, and we should know the riches he gains in our final salvation. Ultimately, this is why we are saved, so that God may have "the riches of his glorious inheritance in the saints."

The second way of taking this statement is that Paul wants us to know the riches that we have in God, the glorious inheritance that God provides to the saints. This is the view taken by John Chrysostom, John Calvin, Charles Hodge, B. F. West-

cott, D. Martyn Lloyd-Jones, John Stott, and James Montgomery Boice. The Greek text allows equally for either reading, but I think there is good reason to favor the second
interpretation. First of all, Paul has already mentioned "our
inheritance" in Ephesians 1:14, as it is guaranteed by the Holy
Spirit. It would be most likely that he is speaking of the same
thing now in his prayer. Second, in his similar prayer at the
beginning of Colossians, which in many ways parallels the book
of Ephesians, Paul writes that God "has qualified you to share
in the inheritance of the saints in light" (Col. 1:12).

The point, then, is that Paul prays for us to know the
riches of the glory of the inheritance that God has for us in
Christ. Having begun with reference to the beginning of our
salvation—our calling—Paul now wants us to apprehend the
reality of what awaits us at the end.

Notice how excited Paul is getting, as he starts here to
pile up superlatives. First, our inheritance is so abundant that
he refers to it as riches. God says in Proverbs 8:18–19:

> Riches and honor are with me,
>   enduring wealth and righteousness.
> My fruit is better than gold, even fine gold,
>   and my yield than choice silver.

Second, it is an inheritance of glory. Daniel 12:3 says, "Those
who are wise shall shine like the brightness of the sky above;
and those who turn many to righteousness, like the stars forever and ever." Paul writes in Romans 8:16–17, "We are children of God, and if children, then heirs—heirs of God and
fellow heirs with Christ, provided we suffer with him in order
that we may also be glorified with him." Third, as an inheritance, it is something that is secure. It is not earned but given.
Once received it is held as a possession by right. Fourth, it is
an inheritance in the saints, that is, held in communion with

all the company of the redeemed. The joys we know now as we share in our gifts and graces, in worship and prayer, in the fellowship of faith, will all pale before the inheritance we have together in the fellowship of the riches of God's glory.

Since Paul so greatly wants our hearts to see these riches, we should dwell on what we have a right to expect at the end of our Christian journey. While we wait we are sustained by hope, but at the end hope will give way to full possession. And what will we then have?

Our inheritance includes a perfect justification in the day of God's final judgment. All of us will be present before the great white throne for a final division. To one side those who have not come to Christ for salvation will go to the condemnation their sins have deserved. To the other side will go the sheep who are saved by the Good Shepherd's blood, to be led by him forever beside streams of living water. What a treasure it will be then to hear the words of Romans 8:1, "There is therefore now no condemnation for those who are in Christ Jesus."

If that is not enough, there is more. We not only will be acquitted of guilt but also will be perfected in holiness. Christians are to anticipate the day when we will no longer contend with sinful motives, with an impure heart, with vile, angry, and selfish thoughts. Thomas Watson writes, "Death smites a believer as the angel did Peter, and made his chains fall off (Acts 12:7). Believers at death are made perfect in holiness. . . . Oh! what a blessed privilege is this, to be without spot or wrinkle; to be purer than the sunbeams; to be as free from sin as the angels!"[2] Hebrews 12:23 speaks of those in heaven as "the spirits of the righteous made perfect," and that is what we will be.

D. Martyn Lloyd-Jones tells a story about Philip Henry, the father of the great Bible commentator Matthew Henry. He had fallen in love with a young lady who belonged to a much higher social class but who was a fervent Christian. Her parents were unhappy about the match and questioned her, "This man Philip Henry, where has he come from?" The woman's reply was priceless: "I don't know where he has come from, but I know where he is going."[3] That is true of all who have come to God through faith in Jesus Christ. Wherever we are from, we are going to an inheritance in heaven the like of which our feeble minds can scarcely conceive.

We see, then, why Paul writes as he does—riches, glory, an inheritance, in the saints! John Chrysostom exclaimed, "What language shall be adequate to express that glory of which the saints shall then be partakers?" There is none, he concludes.[4] The apostle John was similarly overwhelmed. He writes, "Beloved, we are God's children now, and what we will be has not yet appeared; but we know that when he appears we will be like him, because we shall see him as he is" (1 John 3:2). Our inheritance ultimately is God in Christ; he gives himself to us even as he takes us to himself. With renewed eyes we will see in heaven what only the eyes of our hearts can now perceive as the Holy Spirit opens them: the vision of God in his glory, infinite perfection extended to us in infinite love. Revelation 22:4–5 says of us, "They will see his face, and his name will be on their foreheads. And night will be no more. They will need no light of lamp or sun, for the Lord God will be their light, and they will reign forever and ever."

HIS INCOMPARABLY GREAT POWER

Third, Paul wants us to realize "what is the immeasurable greatness of his power toward us who believe." He first directed our attention to the beginning of our Christian life, our calling, and then to the end, our inheritance among the saints. Now he speaks of what we need along the way, power from God to persevere and conquer in the faith.

The apostle Paul is well known for his doctrine of justification by faith apart from works. In Ephesians 2:8–9 we encounter one of his classic expressions of this: "By grace you have been saved through faith. And this is not your own doing; it is the gift of God, not a result of works, so that no one may boast." Because of this, many people fail to appreciate the importance to Paul of good works and godly lives, to which we thus are saved. Carson writes, "Paul cannot be satisfied with a brand of Christianity that is orthodox but dead, rich in the theory of justification but powerless when it comes to transforming people's lives."[5]

Paul's thought on the matter is best stated in Romans 8:3–4, "For God has done what the law, weakened by the flesh, could not do. By sending his own Son in the likeness of sinful flesh and for sin, he condemned sin in the flesh, in order that the righteous requirement of the law might be fulfilled in us, who walk not according to the flesh but according to the Spirit." We cannot be saved by obeying the law because the law is unable to give power to our weak and sinful nature. But it is precisely in this that the gospel is different, so that those who are saved by faith in Christ are then enabled by God's power to keep and obey the law as a result of this salvation by grace alone. This being the case, Paul is eager that we should realize what is the power for this obedience that is available to us in Christ.

As Paul turns to this he falls all over himself in a deluge of words. Ephesians 1:19 employs no fewer than four different words, each of which speaks of God's incomparably great and mighty power. The first is *dynamis,* from which we get "dynamite" and which speaks of raw power to overcome obstacles. The second is *energeia,* from which we get "energy," which speaks of God energizing his people for godliness. Paul uses this same word in Philippians 2:12–13: "Work out your own salvation with fear and trembling, for it is God who works in you, both to will and to work for his good pleasure." God pro-

206

vides power and energy for holiness to his people. The third word, *kratos,* and the fourth, *isxus,* both mean "might" or "strength." Leon Morris summarizes, "Paul is using a multiplicity of words denoting power to bring out the truth that . . . there is mighty power in God and it is a power directed towards the betterment of believers."[6]

In case we have trouble understanding the scope and dimensions of this transforming power, Paul provides for us the supreme analogy, the death and resurrection of Jesus Christ, saying that the power God has for us is "according to the working of his great might that he worked in Christ when he raised him from the dead" (Eph. 1:19–20).

The importance of this point is evidenced by the number of times Paul presses it upon his readers in his various letters. It is not an exaggeration to state that our maturity and growth in the faith utterly requires that we grasp this truth and its reality in our lives. What was your condition before you came to faith? "You were dead in [your] trespasses and sins," Paul writes in Ephesians 2:1. Likewise, Jesus Christ was dead and buried in the grave, suffering his death so that you could be released from yours. Now, by the same power by which he raised Jesus from the dead, God has brought you to spiritual life. Paul goes on in Ephesians 2:4–5, "Because of the great love with which he loved us, even when we were dead in our trespasses, [God] made us alive together with Christ."

It is this very power that is available for your ongoing sanctification. God not only raised Jesus, but, Ephesians 1:20 says, God "seated him at his right hand in the heavenly places." Likewise, God's mighty power will lift you out of your sins and elevate you to where Christ now is.

Paul says the same thing elsewhere in different ways. In Romans 6:8–10, he writes, "Now if we have died with Christ, we believe that we will also live with him. We know that Christ being raised from the dead will never die again; death no longer has dominion over him. For the death he died he died to sin, once for all, but the life he lives he lives to God." Do you see his point? When you look at the history of Jesus Christ in his death and resurrection, you are seeing your spiritual biography in him. He died for sin and rose again by God's power. You were dead in sin but have now been spiritually resurrected in Christ. In Galatians 2:19–20 Paul thus writes, "I have been crucified with Christ. It is no longer I who live, but Christ who lives in me."

Ours is this great transformation, that of Christ's resurrection from death to life, so that "if anyone is in Christ, he is a new creation" (2 Cor. 5:17). It is the spiritual equivalent of what happened when Christ raised Lazarus from the dead. This power comes to us, Paul writes elsewhere, from the God "who gives life to the dead and calls into existence the things that do not exist" (Rom. 4:17).

What, then, is the power in which you are seeking to leave behind your sin and misery? Is it this power from God that Paul would have you see? Do you seek it in God's Word and ask for it in prayer, as Jesus taught us, knowing that as a loving Father God gives "the Holy Spirit to those who ask him" (Luke 11:13)? With what power are you trying to resist temptation, to put off hindrances and besetting sins, to develop godly character and bear godly fruit? Your own? The power of some technique or discipline? The fact is that sin is the greatest power in all this world. No method or power from us or from our world can overcome it. But there is a power from beyond this world that is greater than sin, the power of Almighty God working in the lives of those who seek it from him through Jesus Christ.

This is the Bible's answer to a vital question people want to know. I once spoke to a recent convert who had been reading in the Bible of the kind of life God wants him to live. He asked, bewildered, "How am I supposed to do these things?"

He was grateful to be forgiven through faith in Christ, and he wanted to follow him in obedience, but what was the power to enable him?

This is a matter relevant to us all. How are we, with our selfish hearts and our sinful minds, ever going to follow in the way of Christ? We read, for instance, the description of godly love in 1 Corinthians 13:4–5: "Love is patient and kind. . . . It does not insist on its own way; it is not irritable or resentful." But that runs contrary to every instinct of our hearts. How are we to love like that? Or there is Philippians 2:4–5, which says our attitude should be the same as Christ's, looking after the interests of others and not of our own. The problem is that our minds don't work that way. They are not filled with thoughts of others, but immediately our minds demand that we look after ourselves. The list of these things goes on and on—how am I, still contending with my sinful flesh, to walk in the holiness and love of which I read in Scripture?

The answer is here. What is the power I need? It is "the immeasurable greatness of his power toward us who believe, according to the working of his great might that he worked in Christ when he raised him from the dead and seated him at his right hand in the heavenly places" (Eph. 1:19–20). This is what happens as we walk with Jesus, day by day and year by year, that by the Spirit he sends we "are being transformed into the same image from one degree of glory to another" (2 Cor. 3:18). I pray, writes Paul, that the eyes of your heart may apprehend this power and that it may become real in your life as you trust in Jesus Christ.

A Thousand Sacred Sweets

I mentioned poor king Zedekiah, unable to look upon the marvels of Babylon, its hanging gardens and high parapets. But how much greater a tragedy if we should fail to see with the eyes of our hearts, the eyes of faith, the incomparable vision of all that is ours in Christ. How tragic if we should struggle vainly with sin, not seeking God's power in prayer, not keeping in step with the work of God's Holy Spirit. How impoverished must our lives be if we know nothing of the riches of his glorious inheritance that awaits us in the end? How absent of hope must be our journey if we fail to realize what Paul says about God's calling in Philippians 1:6: "He who began a good work in you will bring it to completion at the day of Jesus Christ."

And yet, when our hearts do lay hold of these wonderful truths, what a difference it makes. It is no surprise that these themes have been among the favorites of great hymn writers. Isaac Watts had the eyes of his heart enlightened, and he wrote wonderfully of salvation in these words:

The men of grace have found,
Glory begun below;
Celestial fruit on earthly ground
From faith and hope may grow.

The hill of Zion yields
A thousand sacred sweets,
Before we reach the heav'nly fields,
Or walk the golden streets.

There shall we see His face
And never, never sin;
There from the rivers of His grace
Drink endless pleasures in.

Then let our songs abound,
And ev'ry tear be dry:
We're marching through Immanuel's ground
To fairer worlds on high.[7]

Doesn't that make the pleasures of sin seem dull and unworthy in comparison? Doesn't it amaze you that anyone would renounce these incomparable blessings for the fleeting pleasures of a dying world? God forbid that any of us should turn away from this salvation that is all of God and from God and to the praise of God's glorious grace. Rather, may he open the eyes of our hearts that we may see, and that, seeing, we might live for him who loves us so.

16

CHRIST EXALTED

Ephesians 1:20–23

*And seated him at his right hand in
the heavenly places, far above all rule and authority
and power and dominion, and above every name that is
named, not only in this age but also in the one to come. And
he put all things under his feet and gave him as head
over all things to the church, which is his body,
the fullness of him who fills all in all.*
—Ephesians 1:20–23

his study brings us to the end of the first chapter of Ephesians, which we have seen to be a carefully organized introduction to the whole epistle. After the opening greeting, it presents two long sentences, the first of which is a great hymn of praise. The second is Paul's prayer of thanks and petition to God for his readers. In this chapter Paul has deftly introduced the themes he is going to develop later. We have at various points observed these: the sovereignty of God; the nature, blessing, and destiny of Christians; and the coordinated efforts of the members of the divine Trinity for our salvation.

This being the case, the note Paul chooses to strike at the chapter's end is undoubtedly significant. Here we encounter the theme that rises above the others and in which they are tied together, namely, the believer's union with the crucified, risen, and exalted Christ.

CHRIST EXALTED

Paul ends this chapter with the same theme on which the Gospel accounts end, the ascension and exaltation of Jesus Christ. Forty days after his resurrection, Jesus was taken up before the disciples, visibly rising into heaven as the Shekinah glory cloud enfolded him. Thus was his earthly ministry concluded and his heavenly reign begun.

The exaltation of Christ is God's ultimate vindication of our Lord. Remember the scene as Jesus was dying on the cross. The religious leaders mocked, "He trusts in God; let God deliver him now, if he desires him. For he said, 'I am the Son of God'" (Matt. 27:43). Here is God's reply. Christ's resurrection and ascension prove beyond a doubt that God accepted Christ's obedient life and especially his death as the sacrifice for our sins. The world despised him, but God exalted him to the highest place, proving that his claims were all true.

Paul presents Christ's exaltation in two terms, first in terms of his exalted dignity. He writes that God "seated him at his right hand in the heavenly places, far above all rule and authority and power and dominion, and above every name that is named, not only in this age but also in the one to come" (Eph. 1:20–21).

214

In his exalted dignity, Jesus is portrayed as seated at the place of honor in heaven. Christians have long understood this to signify his finished work as our Savior. Hebrews 1:3 says, "After making purification for sins, he sat down at the right hand of the Majesty on high." This contrasts with the Jewish priests, who never sat down in the temple. Hebrews 10:11 says, "And every priest stands daily at his service, offering repeatedly the same sacrifices, which can never take away sins." But because Jesus' sacrificial death perfectly satisfied God's justice, God exalted him to sit in the heavenly sanctuary. Furthermore, sitting denotes the dignity that Jesus shares with God. All others stand in God's presence, but Jesus sits with him on the throne. The fact that he is sitting shows that his position and reign are firmly established. This is what Daniel saw in his vision, that

> with the clouds of heaven
> there came one like a son of man,
> and he came to the Ancient of Days
> and was presented before him.
> And to him was given dominion
> and glory and a kingdom,
> that all peoples, nations, and languages
> should serve him;
> his dominion is an everlasting dominion,
> which shall not pass away,
> and his kingdom one
> that shall not be destroyed. (Dan. 7:13–14)

Moreover, Jesus is seated at God's right hand. Kings place someone at their right hand to grant honor and to show participation in their rule. This is the highest place that heaven can afford, and such a place is granted to our Lord Jesus Christ. We have here the fulfillment of Psalm 110:1, which the apostles often used as a proof of Christ's divinity and lordship:

> The LORD says to my Lord:
>   "Sit at my right hand,
> until I make your enemies your footstool."

The writer of Hebrews points out how this shows Christ's supremacy to the angels, writing that he became "as much superior to angels as the name he has inherited is more excellent than theirs" (Heb. 1:4). Paul makes this same point in Ephesians 1:21, placing Jesus "far above all rule and authority and power and dominion, and above every name that is named, not only in this age but also in the one to come." These are designations for spiritual beings. Many commentators see these as different grades and ranks within an angelic hierarchy, although that is not Paul's point. Paul writes here in the same way he earlier spoke of God's mighty power, piling on every conceivable designation. He brings forth every word that is in current usage for a spiritual power, and he places Christ above them all.

Paul is probably also reacting against a superstitious idea current in the area of Ephesus at that time, that angels and other semi-divine spirits have to be placated before we can get to God. This was an early form of what would later be called Gnosticism. Paul's letter to the Colossians, which he sent along with Ephesians, shows his concern about this. In this case, Paul is pointing out that since Christ is exalted over all, any such ideas must fall away before his supremacy. Furthermore, Ephesus was a center of pagan magical activity, in which sorcerers evoked names or titles of various powers. But all these ideas are countered by the exaltation of Christ, to whom believers have access by simple faith. Whatever title or name one can think of, either now or in the future, it pales before the status and honor and privilege given to Christ.

Such is the exalted dignity of Christ in heaven. But Paul also wants us to know that Christ is exalted in his present dominion. It is not merely honor that Jesus has received but royal authority. This is an implication of his sitting at God's right hand. Paul therefore adds in Ephesians 1:22, "And [God] put all things under his feet."

All these rulers and authorities, powers and lords—many of which may have been thought threatening to the Christians in that pagan age—are not only inferior to Christ but also subject to him. The imagery reminds us of Joshua's victory over the five Amorite kings. After their defeat, Joshua brought forth the five chieftains. Calling his generals, he said, "Come near; put your feet on the necks of these kings" (Josh. 10:24). It was a sign of their subjugation to his power and was a prelude to their execution. That is the situation of every hostile power, circumstance, and danger to which we are exposed—they are under Christ's feet, all our enemies soon to be put away.

During his earthly ministry, our Lord stood before the storm. He commanded, "Peace, be still!" and the winds and the waves obeyed. How much more, now that he is enthroned in heavenly power, can he govern the circumstances that threaten us, allowing them only to do us ultimate good. While on earth, Jesus cast out demons; we see the demons cringing before him in the Gospels. How much more now must they fear him since he is exalted with authority in heaven. Knowing this ought to motivate our prayers and empower our faith.

Before his ascension, Jesus said, "All authority in heaven and on earth has been given to me" (Matt. 28:18). We need to remember this in a time when Christ's reign is mainly associated with his second coming. Too many Christians look only to the future for Jesus' reign on earth to begin. Jesus' return in glory will put an end to all conflict against him. But even now, while the battle still rages, Jesus reigns over heaven and earth. He is glorified now; he wears the crown even as we

217

serve him here, no less than he will in the day of his glorious return. And the divine power that raised him there, that delivered him from the agony of the cross to the triumph of his exaltation in honor and dominion, is the same power he employs to lift us from our sins and from power of this evil world so that we might follow Jesus and join him where he is.

CHRIST AND HIS CHURCH

Paul is directing our attention to the exalted station of Christ so that we will trust and honor him but also to help us understand all that it means to be joined to him in faith. To this end, he adds, in Ephesians 1:22–23, that God "gave him as head over all things to the church, which is his body, the fullness of him who fills all in all." Paul's first point was that Jesus is exalted over all, his and our enemies under his feet. His second point is that the exalted Christ is given to the church as its head, ruling on its behalf, while the church is given to him as his body.

The relationship between Christ and his people is so rich and complex that Paul uses several metaphors in Ephesians to describe it. In Ephesians 2 he describes us as God's household or family, and then as a building that God is erecting on the firm foundation of Christ. In Ephesians 5 he says the union of a husband and wife illustrates the mystery of our union with Christ. But the chief designation he employs is that of a head with its body.

This points to the organic union between Christ and his church. A human being is not just a collection of parts but an integrated whole. Such is our spiritual union together with Christ. The head and the body are one, inseparable. Paul also has in mind Christ's ruling or governing function over the church, in the same way that the head rules the body. Unlike Christ's enemies, who are ruled by force, we are ruled the way the head governs the body. His rule is not upon us but within us. This tells us, by the way, that we must reject all schemes that place a human leader atop the church, as with the Roman Catholic Church and the pope. The church has only one head, who lives and reigns forever, Jesus Christ. We are each in personal, organic union with Christ. Further, Paul's metaphor suggests that the head is the source of life and vitality for the body, just as the nervous system of the brain conveys energy and activity to the various body parts. Jesus made this point, comparing himself with a vine that gives life to the branches. "Apart from me," he explained, "you can do nothing" (John 15:5).

This teaching has the most profound implications for the life and work of the church. It means that whatever the church is doing, Christ is doing. Realizing his holy dignity and glory ought to restrain us from worldly or otherwise unworthy practices, especially in our worship services. Jesus' reaction to the worldliness and sin of the seven churches that received letters from him in Revelation 2 and 3 shows this clearly enough. "Repent," he commanded them. "If not, I will come to you and remove your lampstand from its place, unless you repent" (Rev. 2:5).

Likewise, if we are in union with Christ, he will rule us as the head rules the body. But how is this realized? It is as the church preaches and obeys the Bible, making God's Word our charter and measuring stick. If our churches are instead taking their direction from secular techniques and church marketing consultants, whose prescriptions so often run directly contrary to the teaching of Christ's Word, it is hard to see how we can continue to consider ourselves in union with Christ.

Again, we said that since Christ is the head and we are the body, then he is the source of our life and vitality. But how does this take place? Jesus showed us plainly in the matter of his apostles. Acts 1:8 tells us that before his ascension, our Lord promised them, "You will receive power when the Holy Spirit has come upon you, and you will be my witnesses." It is by the Holy Spirit that Jesus sends us spiritual life and power. This being the case, we should pray for the working of the Spirit, and we should keep in step with the Spirit as he convicts us to new obedience to God's Word.

It is in these ways that Christ's headship is manifested in the life of churches and individual Christians today—by being with us in all that we do, by giving direction through his authoritative and sufficient Word, and by sending the Holy Spirit to enlighten and enliven us so that we can do his will.

CHRIST EXALTED FOR THE CHURCH

In this context Paul makes an amazing statement that shows why all this matters for us. Ephesians 1:22 says that God "gave him as head over all things to the church." This Jesus, exalted in his heavenly dignity and universal dominion, with all things under his feet and all glory attached to his throne, is given by God to us the church.

We often speak about God's gift to us at Christmastime. In the birth of the baby Jesus, God gave to us his only begotten Son. Or, we talk this way about Christ's death. God in his grace gave Jesus to die in our place. But we seldom speak this way about Jesus' ascension into heaven. And yet, Paul reminds us, this is the culminating gift, the enthronement of him who was born in the lowly manger to enter into our race, who died for us and rose again. In his ascension into heavenly glory and power Jesus' work was brought to triumphant fulfillment. And no less than in the birth of Christ, no less than in his death, God has given him to us. If his birth brings us solace, if his death brings us peace, then Christ's ascension, his taking up the throne for us, ought to give us a final confidence and joy and hope that nothing can ever shake. It was because God gave the exalted Christ to us, as he gave the humble Christ to us, that Paul could write in Romans 8:39 that nothing "will be able to separate us from the love of God in Christ Jesus our Lord."

I want to point out three specific implications of God's gift to us of the exalted and enthroned Lord Jesus.

First, this is a great proof of the assurance of our salvation. Jesus Christ is enthroned forever above all powers and dominions at the right hand of God. It is a man, a human being, who sits upon that throne. He is inseparably joined to us as the head to his body. Surely, then, our salvation is utterly assured. We are like Joseph's brothers, who came to Egypt only to find their long-lost brother enthroned over the mighty foreign land. That is what we shall find in heaven, that one of us, even he who offered himself for us, is seated in the place of honor and power. He sits enthroned in a human body marked by the wounds he suffered for us. This proves that our sins are put away forever and that we who trust in him will certainly find a place with him there.

Furthermore, our every foe has been conquered by the exalted Christ. In his death, resurrection, and ascension he has subdued all his foes and ours, including sin, the world, the devil, and death. We may now face all of these without fear. We must still contend with these enemies, with people and powers that tempt and afflict and oppose us. But they are enemies he has already subdued. Our present conflict is with defeated foes. Instead of truly threatening our salvation, they are made by Christ to be instruments of our sanctification and growth, enemies Christ allows to go only far enough to do us good in our struggles as we learn to trust in him. "In the world you will have tribulation," he told the disciples. "But take heart; I have overcome the world" (John 16:33).

The second implication is to see what Paul is driving at when he speaks of the power that is available to us because Christ is exalted. God gave him as head over everything to the church. Therefore what aid could we need that is beyond his ability to

221

give? What obstacle is so great that he cannot remove it? What calling have we received that he cannot supply the power to fulfill? What challenge must we endure, what temptation or trial do we face, with what sin are we burdened but that Christ cannot overcome it as he works in us with his almighty power?

The great illustration of this truth is the apostle Paul. What kind of man wrote this great letter to the Ephesians? He was the greatest sinner in all the world, by his own assessment, the harshest critic and most hateful persecutor of Christians. But how easy it was for Christ to turn this violent Pharisee into the great apostle of grace, the man who did more to establish the early church than anyone else. Christ changed his mind, changed his heart, changed his life. Paul, then named Saul of Tarsus, was traveling to Damascus to persecute the Christians there, having worn out the Christians in Jerusalem and needing fresh victims. Luke tells us what happened:

> Now as he went on his way, he approached Damascus, and suddenly a light from heaven flashed around him. And falling to the ground he heard a voice saying to him, "Saul, Saul, why are you persecuting me?" And he said, "Who are you, Lord?" And he said, "I am Jesus, whom you are persecuting. But rise and enter the city, and you will be told what you are to do." (Acts 9:3–6)

That was all it took, and Paul became the greatest apostle there ever was. On what basis, then, do you doubt that the exalted Christ can make use of your life, deliver you from your sins, change your heart and mind and life? He will do so, according to his particular plan and purpose for you, if you are joined to him by faith and if you seek to do his will.

Another example comes from Paul's plea in 2 Corinthians 12. Paul writes of receiving a thorn in his flesh, "a messenger of Satan to harass me" (v. 7). He couldn't stand it. He couldn't take it any longer, whatever it was. Three times he pleaded for the Lord to take it away. But God did not take it away. Instead, he gave Paul power to endure it cheerfully. He said, "My grace is sufficient for you, for my power is made perfect in weakness" (2 Cor. 12:9). Paul, who earlier complained that it was unbearable, replied, "Therefore I will boast all the more gladly of my weaknesses, so that the power of Christ may rest upon me. For the sake of Christ, then, I am content with weaknesses, insults, hardships, persecutions and calamities. For when I am weak, then I am strong" (2 Cor. 12:9–10). We think that Christ's power has let us down or is disproved if we have any troubles, any temptations, any weaknesses that have not been done away with. But he says that his power enables us to endure in them by faith so that he may be glorified in our weakness. Therefore D. Martyn Lloyd-Jones writes:

> As we contemplate life and all its difficulties, and as we are tempted by Satan to feel that all is impossible, and that we cannot go on because we are so weak and the difficulties so baffling, we must remind ourselves of this truth and say: I am a very small and unimportant member, but I am a member of the body of Christ; I am "in him," and therefore, whatever may be true of me personally, the life of the Head is in me. . . . I am in touch with Him, His vital energy is in me. . . . As our eyes are opened to this truth we can take fresh courage, and take up our task again and say: In Christ I cannot fail, I must not fail, He will not allow me to fail.[1]

The third implication has to do with the church. People don't think much of the church, even Christians. The church is someplace they go to get something for themselves, to get a lift, to get some help, to make some decent friends. The world looks on the church as something insignificant and weak. The great things in this world deal with skyscrapers and stock markets, rising and falling empires. This was especially a danger for the fledgling churches of Paul's day, which were viewed, and might have viewed themselves, as an insignificant cult among a sea of religious groups. But here we see that the church cannot be rightly understood apart from seeing the exalted Christ, who rules over every power and all of history, and its relationship to him. The church is the preeminent institution in all the world because it is the body of him who is seated at God's right hand in the heavenly realms. Only the church, among all institutions in this world, will endure forever, its accomplishments blazing forever when all else has passed away.

There is therefore no greater privilege than membership in the church. There is no greater calling than Christians' calling to offer their gifts and talents, time and money to the work of the church. A Christian who gives all his energy to his job, who uses her talents only for personal gain, who spends his money all on himself, neglecting the work of the church, which will last forever, is a fool. Such a person does not recognize that the church is the body, the temple, the bride of him who is exalted on high. In the end it is what Christ has done through the church that will matter most, will most shine in glory, and will have been most worth the offering of our lives. Therefore Christians who are not involved in a ministry of the church, who do not pray regularly for the church's work, who take but never give to the church, should ask themselves if they understand what this life is about, if they see this Christ who is exalted, and if so what kind of response is appropriate to that realization.

THE CHURCH AS THE FULLNESS OF CHRIST

Paul concludes with one of the most remarkable statements in all the New Testament. He describes the church as "the fullness of him who fills all in all" (Eph. 1:23).

There are two ways in which the church may be understood as "the fullness" of Christ, and scholars are divided on the issue. The first and most accepted view is that Paul means the church is filled with and by Christ. The advantage of this view is that it fits with what we find elsewhere in the Bible. Andrew Lincoln explains, "Everywhere else Christ is portrayed as actively filling believers rather than being filled by them . . . [otherwise] a deficiency in his person would be implied."[2] Charles Hodge takes this view, explaining, "As the body is filled or pervaded by the soul, so the church is filled by the Spirit of Christ; or, as God of old dwelt in the temple, and filled it with his glory, so Christ now dwells in his church and fills it with his presence."[3]

All of that is true, but I think the second view better fits what Paul is particularly saying here. Paul's writing here is very bold, and we should not shrink from being equally bold; he frankly says that the church fills Christ, even as Christ is the One who fills all things in every way.

In what sense, then, might we say that we are the fullness of Christ? It is true that, being God, the Lord Jesus is self-sufficient and does not need us or anything else. He is hardly an empty or half-empty vessel! But as our mediator and redeemer, he is joined to the church as the head to the body, and in that sense he requires us to be complete. That is the straightforward meaning of Paul's words in this verse. First he names us the body, with Christ as head, and then designates the church as the fullness of him who fills all things. John Calvin accordingly writes:

> This is the highest honor of the Church, that, unless He is united to us, the Son of God reckons Himself in some measure imperfect. What an encouragement it is for us to hear, that, not until He has us as one with Himself, is He complete in all His parts, or does He wish to be regarded as whole![4]

That is the highest ground of our hope for salvation. Arthur Pink says, "There cannot be a Redeemer without redeemed, a Shepherd without sheep, a Bridegroom without a bride, a living Head without a living body. He is *her* fullness as the Lord of life and grace; she is *His* fullness since by means of the glory He has put upon her He will hereafter be magnified."[5] That being the case, we see why Christ so loves his church and why he secures for us a place where he is and provides for us his power. Even this filling of himself is his work, his filling of all things in every way to the praise of his glorious grace. He says, "Because I live, you also will live" (John 14:19).

ALL THINGS TOGETHER IN CHRIST

In Ephesians 1:10, Paul describes God's ultimate purpose as "to unite all things in [Christ], things in heaven and things on earth." It is with this idea that he now wraps up the chapter, with Christ exalted over all, filling and being filled. This great theme ties in with all the other themes touched upon in this chapter. They are all brought together "in Christ," an expression Paul has used no fewer than eleven times in Ephesians 1.

First, we have considered in this chapter the incomparable blessings that belong to our salvation. These blessings are found in Christ. Their source is the exalted Christ, who is the head of the body, his church, and who sits enthroned at God's right hand above all other rule and authority, power and dominion. Paul said in Ephesians 1:3 that God "has blessed us in Christ with every spiritual blessing in the heavenly places." We see now how that is, for the heavenly realms is where Christ is exalted in honor and in power.

Another theme Paul has emphasized is the sovereignty of God. God ordained our salvation "according to the purpose of him who works all things according to the counsel of his will" (Eph. 1:11). But the ultimate expression of God's sovereignty is the exaltation of Christ and of the church with him. Now it is Christ who wields that scepter for our sake. "All our days," writes D. A. Carson, "fall within the sweep of the sovereignty of one who wears a human face, a thorn-shadowed face. All of God's sovereignty is mediated through one who was crucified on my behalf."[6] The heavenly rule is exercised for our benefit and blessing. God's sovereignty can no longer be considered a dark and ominous threat, but it is now a cause for the greatest gratitude and confidence and an incentive to the most expectant prayers.

Finally, we have often noted what this chapter says about the identity and nature of a Christian. What is a Christian? we have asked. Here is the ultimate answer. A Christian is one who is joined to Jesus Christ through faith, receiving the redeeming benefit of his death on the cross, who is a member of the church that is his body, thus receiving assurance and awesome power for salvation. Therefore, the final verses of this great chapter tell us that what matters above all else is how we stand with regard to Christ. The world rejected him—that we know. They spurned his grace, nailed him to the cross, and consigned him to the grave. But God

> raised him from the dead and seated him at his right hand in the heavenly places, far above all rule and authority and power and dominion, and above every name that is named, not only in this age but also in the one to come. And he put all things under his feet and gave him as head over all things to the church, which is his body, the fullness of him who fills all in all.

Therefore, the destiny of every individual, every one of us, is determined by how we stand in relation to Jesus Christ. If we stand in indifference or in opposition, we will be placed under his feet in defeated subjection, soon to be judged and condemned for our sins. But if we come to him in grateful faith, as the One who loved us and gave himself for us, he will be our Savior and our Lord, we will be his people, we will be blessed by him forever, filling and being filled, so that his exaltation might be completed in our exaltation and praise unto him.

To him be glory in the church, throughout all generations, forever and ever. Amen.

17

Prayer and the Sovereignty of God

Ephesians 1:15–23

*For this reason, because I have heard of your faith
in the Lord Jesus and your love toward all the saints, I do not
cease to give thanks for you, remembering you in my prayers.*
—Ephesians 1:15–16

The last study brought us to the end of Ephesians 1, which is one of the great chapters in the New Testament. In conclusion, I want to look back over the prayer that ends this chapter and consider the matter of prayer and the sovereignty of God.

There are two reasons to do this. The first is that many people have concerns over this matter. If God is as sovereign as Paul depicts him in this chapter, then the whole realm of human activity—and especially prayer—seems to come into question. My second purpose is to use this discussion as a summary of this marvelous chapter, which presents a great salvation that rests secure on God's sovereign grace and leads us into a living relationship with him through faith in Jesus Christ.

If God Is Sovereign, Why Should We Pray?

The question is, Do prayer and the sovereignty of God go together? If God is sovereign in all things, if God has ordained everything in advance according to his predetermined plan, then what is the point of prayer? Why should we tell God our needs and cry to him from our hearts if he knows all things in advance? For some, this is a problem that calls the whole matter of God's sovereignty into question. "We know God wants us to pray," they argue, "and the idea of a sovereign, predestinating God seems incompatible with prayer."

One way to realize that prayer must be compatible with God's sovereignty is to consider the example of the apostle Paul. Throughout his many letters, Paul repeatedly and deliberately emphasizes God's sovereignty. This is what we have found in Ephesians 1. In Ephesians 1:4, Paul says that God "chose us . . . before the foundation of the world." Ephesians 1:5 adds that he predestined us for adoption into his family. Ephesians 1:11 teaches that we were made heirs "having been predestined according to the purpose of him who works all things according to the counsel of his will." It is hard to imagine what stronger terminology Paul could possibly use to convey the idea that we are saved by God's sovereign grace. Indeed, Paul does not limit God's sovereignty to the sphere of salvation but says in Acts 17:26, "He made from one man every nation of mankind to live on all the face of the earth, having determined allotted periods and the boundaries of their dwelling place." God's sovereignty is unrestrained in

Paul's thinking; it is unequivocal and total. As God said through Isaiah:

> I am God, and there is no other;
>   I am God, and there is none like me,
> declaring the end from the beginning
>   and from ancient times things not yet done,
> saying, "My counsel shall stand,
>   and I will accomplish all my purpose."
>   (Isa. 46:9–10)

Like Isaiah in the Old Testament, it is Paul in the New Testament who is especially identified with the sovereignty of God.

The question therefore arises, Did Paul's belief in God's complete sovereignty cause him to lose interest in prayer? Because God is in control did Paul think little of the Christian's activity and responsibility? If, as many people say, prayer and the sovereignty of God are incompatible, we should expect to see this play out in Paul's example more than in any other. But not only is Paul noted for his teaching of God's sovereignty, he is also eminent as a man of prayer. Not only Ephesians but all his letters overflow with prayer like flowers blossoming in a garden. Furthermore, he often prays with direct reference to God's sovereignty. In 2 Thessalonians 2:13, he writes, "We ought always to give thanks to God for you, brothers beloved by the Lord, because God chose you as the first fruits to be saved."

We are confronted, then, with this situation: the apostle most noted for teaching the highest view of God's total sovereignty was not thereby discouraged from praying, just as his belief in predestination did not lessen his zeal for evangelistic outreach and preaching. Instead, while strongly emphasizing God's sovereign election, Paul was singular in zeal for evangelism and prayer. C. Samuel Storms is surely right when he concludes, "That Paul should speak with perfect ease of both sovereign election and prayer . . . requires that we view them as theologically (and logically) compatible. Divine sovereignty does not preempt prayer, nor does prayer render God's choice contingent."[1]

We will find the same situation if we turn to the greater example of our Lord Jesus Christ. Think, for instance, of Jesus' prediction of Peter's denial. "I tell you, Peter," he said, "the rooster will not crow this day, until you deny three times that you know me" (Luke 22:34). Jesus' espousal of divine sovereignty and foreknowledge is shown by his advance certainty of minute details such as the number of Peter's denials and crowing of the rooster. Jesus also knew that Peter would repent and be restored. And yet none of this sovereign foreknowledge deterred him from prayer. In Luke 22:31–32 Jesus says, "Simon, Simon . . . I have prayed for you that your faith may not fail."

GOD'S SOVEREIGNTY AS THE REASON FOR PRAYER

Paul's example gives us sufficient reason to view prayer and God's sovereignty as fully compatible. But this prayer which concludes Ephesians 1 offers us particularly keen insight into the relationship between the two. This passage from Ephesians 1:15–23 specifically tells us three things about prayer and the sovereignty of God. It says that because God is sovereign, we have every reason to pray, we have every need to pray, and we have every encouragement to pray.

First is God's sovereignty as a reason for prayer. This is Paul's explicit statement in Ephesians 1:15–16: "For this reason, because I have heard of your faith in the Lord Jesus and your love toward all the saints, I do not cease to give thanks for you, remembering you in my prayers." "For this reason" looks back on all that Paul had just taught, namely, God's sovereign grace in Christ. It is in light of this that it occurs to him to pray for his readers. He thinks of them, recalls their faith and love, and, reflecting on God's sovereignty, exclaims, "I have not stopped giving thanks for you."

So, if God is sovereign, why should we pray? First and foremost, we pray to thank God for the blessings of his sovereign grace. This is a vital reason for our prayer: to thank God for what he has done in our lives, knowing it is all of him, and also for what he has done for others. Indeed, this recalls Paul's beginning to the whole letter: "Praise be to the God and Father of our Lord Jesus Christ, who has blessed us in the heavenly realms with every spiritual blessing in Christ" (Eph. 1:3). That is what he does in prayer. He praises and thanks God for all that he has done for us in Christ.

It is precisely because God is sovereign, because the salvation of these people came from his pure choice, that God alone is praised for their salvation. Were salvation based not on God's sovereignty, but at least in part on our supposedly free wills, then the praise would not all go to God. But Paul does not praise and thank the Ephesians for their faith and love, nor does he credit their pastors or even himself. Since God's sovereign grace is the cause of their salvation, all the praise and thanks go to him, and therefore Paul has a reason to pray to God.

Many people today reject Paul's doctrine of God's sovereignty, and one result is a diminishing emphasis on prayer in our churches. Toward the end of his ministry, James Montgomery Boice began to notice that in so many of the churches he visited, less and less time in corporate worship was being given to prayer. What prayer there was was tacked onto the service and dealt almost exclusively with requests for people who were sick and other needs. Christians were not reflecting on God's attributes or God's works in their prayers, nor were they praising or thanking him. Reflecting on the great Refor-

233

mation theme of *soli deo gloria*—to God alone be the glory—Boice wrote this about those who deny God's sovereignty: "They want to glorify God . . . but they cannot say 'to God *alone* be glory,' because they insist on mixing human will power or ability with . . . gospel grace."[2]

As long as we believe that salvation results from human sovereignty, from human choice and will and decision, denying the Bible's teaching that people contribute only their sin and that God saves us by his sovereign, almighty grace alone, we will continue to focus on what we are doing and ought to do, neglecting prayer and the giving of praise and thanks to God. If ultimately it is human will that decides salvation, then we will appeal to humans and seek to please them instead of God. In contrast to the man-centered spirit of our age, Paul's grand view of God's sovereignty supplies a compelling reason for us to pray, namely, to give praise and thanks to God for his grace.

GOD'S SOVEREIGNTY AND THE NEED FOR PRAYER

God's sovereignty also provides the need for prayer, as this passage shows. Paul asks that "the God of our Lord Jesus Christ, the Father of glory, may give you a spirit of wisdom and of revelation in the knowledge of him, having the eyes of your hearts enlightened" (Eph. 1:17–18).

Since God is sovereign, we must pray to him because salvation wholly depends on his gracious working, on the spiritual resources we cannot create but he is able to provide. Specifically, Paul realizes that we utterly depend on God giving his Holy Spirit to enliven and illuminate our hearts, to make us spiritually receptive, to open blind eyes to the light that is shining. First Corinthians 2:14 says, "The natural person does not accept the things of the Spirit of God, for they are folly to him, and he is not able to understand them because they are spiritually discerned." This is why Paul so often prays for the conversion of unbelievers and for the spiritual growth of believers, because the work of God's Spirit is necessary for both. Likewise, we must pray to the sovereign God for ourselves and for others, beseeching the Spirit's quickening and illuminating work.

This raises a question: Does prayer change God's will? Is God's mind or attitude or purpose altered by our prayers? To understand prayer rightly, and its relationship to God's sovereignty, we must realize that the answer to this question is no. Prayer does not change God's will.

There are people today who insist that if prayer does not change God's mind or will, then there is no need to pray and the Bible's emphasis on prayer is a sham. But far from being outraged at the idea that prayer does not change God's will, Christians should be profoundly grateful. God is, after all, all-wise. What wisdom might we contribute to his thinking that would produce a superior understanding? Likewise, God is completely holy. Do we wish that we, being sinful and corrupt, could exert a moral influence on God's holiness? And what sort of influence do we think it might be? God's mind is informed by omniscience—perfect knowledge of all things, past, present, and future. Do we wish him to change his mind based on our ignorance? For all these reasons, we should be glad that God is sovereign and that our prayers do not change his mind.

The Bible makes clear that God's will is not changed by prayer or anything else, having been established in eternity. Isaiah 46:11 says, "I have spoken, and I will bring it to pass; I have purposed, and I will do it." In Ephesians 1:11, Paul tells us that God "works all things according to the counsel of his will." He asks, in Romans 11:34, "Who has known the mind of the Lord, or who has been his counselor?" The answer is no one. Christian leaders glibly talk of our prayers shaping God's policy today, but if God's purpose is an eternal one, as Paul insists, then his policy is not being shaped today.[3] Our folly does not dictate to God's wisdom. Our sinfulness does not direct his holiness. Our ignorance does not overrule his perfect knowledge. If our prayers changed God's will, then we would be sovereign, not he, and his will could no longer be described as Paul does in Romans 12:2, "his good, pleasing and perfect will" (NIV).

Prayer does not change God's will. Now let me ask the question a different way: Do our prayers change things? Are there things that happen that would not have happened had we not prayed or if we had prayed for something different? Here the answer is yes. Our prayers do change things, because God is sovereign and has ordained prayer as a means to the ends that he also has ordained. While prayer does not change God's will or plan, prayer is used by God within his will and plan. It is in this sense that he says to all his people, "Pray to me, and I will hear you" (Jer. 29:12).

Even if prayer did not change circumstances, it would still be worthwhile to pray, first to praise God, but also because prayer changes us. Prayer changes our attitude to circumstances that God may not wish to change. Paul says, "In everything by prayer and supplication with thanksgiving let your requests be made known to God. And the peace of God, which surpasses all understanding, will guard your hearts and your minds in Christ Jesus" (Phil. 4:6–7). That alone is an important reason why we need to pray. People who insist that prayer matters only if God grants our wishes fail to appreciate the importance of adoration and the value of the peace God gives.

But prayer goes beyond changing us: it changes things, it changes events, it changes outcomes. Why? Because the God to whom we pray is sovereign—he is able to do all things—and he has ordained prayer as a means by which all he has ordained will come to pass. Therefore we should pray for all our needs, for help, for relief, for God's power to overcome dangers and temptations and to help us in our witness and ministry, because it is through our prayers that God intends to provide these things. As Martin Luther said, "Prayer is not overcoming God's reluctance, but laying hold of His willingness."[4]

Storms offers an example of how prayer serves as a means God has provided to accomplish the ends he has ordained. Suppose God decided that a man named Gary will be saved through faith in Christ on August 8. Suppose, also, that unbeknownst to me God wills to bring him to faith in response to my prayer for Gary on August 7. Storms asks:

> Does this mean that God's will for Gary's salvation on the eighth might fail should I forget or refuse to pray on the seventh? No. We must remember that God has decreed or willed my praying on the seventh for Gary's salvation, which he intends to effect on the eighth. God does not will the end, that is, Gary's salvation on the eighth, apart from the means, that is, my prayer on the seventh. . . . From a human perspective, it may rightly be said that God's will for Gary is dependent upon me and my prayers, as long as it is understood that God, by an infallible decree, has secured and guaranteed my prayers as an instrument with no less certainty than he has secured and guaranteed Gary's faith as an end.[5]

Why, some then will ask, should I bother praying, if it is all decreed by God? The answer is that I do not know what God has ordained until it happens. Having Gary's salvation on my heart, what else should I do but pray and use every other opportunity to lead him to faith and salvation, trusting that God will bless these means as he is so often glad to do?

Prayer does not change God, but it does change things, according to God's eternal counsel and sovereign will. Therefore Paul sees an urgent need for prayer, and he prays that

God will send the Holy Spirit to lead the Ephesians into a deeper knowledge of God and power for newness of life.

GOD'S SOVEREIGNTY AS AN
ENCOURAGEMENT TO PRAYER

First, God's sovereignty gives us every reason to pray, as well as every need to pray. Finally, we have every encouragement to pray, because Christ is exalted over all, exercising God's royal sovereignty for the church.

We shall utterly fail to grasp Paul's emphasis in this chapter unless we realize that God's sovereignty is exercised in Christ and through Christ for our salvation. This means that if you want to know that God has chosen you for salvation, then you must come to Jesus Christ in faith. But it also means that if you belong to Christ, then God's sovereignty is exercised by him for your benefit. This is why Paul ends the chapter by showing us Christ exalted: "He raised him from the dead and seated him at his right hand in the heavenly places, far above all rule and authority and power and dominion, and above every name that is named, not only in this age but also in the one to come" (Eph. 1:20–21). God exalted Christ for a reason, namely, Paul continues, to be "head over all things [for] the church, which is his body, the fullness of him who fills all in all" (Eph. 1:22–23).

When we bow our heads and lift our hearts to God in the name of Jesus, that is the name of the One who sits at God's right hand in glory and power. The Son of God is enthroned as a man, knowing all too well what it is to sorrow and suffer, to have need of God's help, of God's grace, of God's mercy, of God's power in the Holy Spirit. Hebrews 4:15–16 reflects on this: "For we do not have a high priest who is unable to sympathize with our weaknesses, but one who in every respect has been tempted as we are, yet without sin. Let us then with confidence draw near to the throne of grace, that we may receive mercy and find grace to help in time of need."

Since God has exalted his Son, the man Jesus Christ, to the place of sovereignty, we are encouraged by his ability to understand our needs. Furthermore, since this is the same Lord Jesus who loved us and gave his life for our sins, we can be sure of his willingness to employ his divine power and authority for our sakes. Our prayers are received into hands that were pierced for us. What greater encouragement could we have about the welcome our prayers will receive in the courts of heaven? Paul reasons in Romans 5:10, "If while we were enemies we were reconciled to God by the death of his Son, much more, now that we are reconciled, shall we be saved by his life."

The story is told of a Civil War soldier who went to the White House with a pressing need he thought only the president could meet. To his dismay, he found a great number of people seeking an audience and a staff of assistants whose job it was to keep them out. Dejected, the soldier fell into a seat, where a young boy came up to him and asked him why he felt so sad. The man replied, "I came a long way to see the president, but now I realize I won't be able to." The little boy grabbed him by the hand and led him past the guards and the staff of assistants, through a number of doors and into the Oval Office where the president was working. "Father," the boy said, "this soldier needs your help." Abraham Lincoln put down his pen, looked up, and said, "Certainly, my son. Now, my friend, what can I do to help you?" That is what it means to us that God's Son, Jesus Christ, is there in heaven, exalted for us, so that we will always have access in prayer to the heavenly Father.

THE SCEPTER RAISED

If God is sovereign, why should we pray? We have every reason to pray because of the thanks we owe to God for his sovereign grace. We have every need to pray because of our whole reliance on the work of his Holy Spirit. But above all this, we have every encouragement to pray because of our assurance of God's favor in Christ, his Son and our Savior, who grants us unfailing access to the Father and whom God has established as head over all for the sake of the church.

There is a story in the Bible that speaks of the great privilege of this access and favor. The story is that of Esther, the Jewish girl who became queen of Persia. The Book of Esther deals with a plot by the evil official Haman to have the Jews persecuted. Godly Mordecai, Esther's uncle, who had incurred Haman's wrath by refusing to bow to him, appealed for Esther to use her influence to protect God's people. Esther was afraid to act, because one could approach the king in his inner court only if first summoned by him. Anyone who approached the king without being summoned was required by law to be put to death (Esther 4:11). The person could be spared only if the king, seeing him or her, extended his golden scepter, admitting the petitioner into his royal presence. After three days of prayer and fasting, Esther summoned the resolve to go forward. First she put on her royal robes, and only then did she go into the king's inner chamber and stand before him. Esther 5:2–3 tells us what happened:

> When the king saw Queen Esther standing in the court, she won favor in his sight, and he held out to Esther the golden scepter that was in his hand. Then Esther approached and touched the tip of the scepter. And the king said to her, "What is it, Queen Esther? What is your request? It shall be given you, even to the half of my kingdom."

If that is the response of a pagan monarch toward his wife, how much more can we expect when we appear in

Christ's name before the throne of our heavenly Father? Like Esther, we must be careful to come in the robe God has given us, even the perfect righteousness of Jesus Christ, imputed to us through faith in his blood. So dressed, as Christ's bride, we shall surely be precious in his sight. And, with our Savior Jesus enthroned forever as Lord over all, we will surely find the scepter permanently raised for us. The wrath of God's law was put aside once for all at the cross, the veil removed that once kept us out from God's presence, and the scepter of access is now extended to us forever. As Paul writes later in this epistle, "Through him," that is, Christ, we "have access . . . to the Father" (Eph. 2:18).

Count Zinzendorf wrote,

> *Jesus, thy blood and righteousness*
> *My beauty are, my glorious dress;*
> *'Midst flaming worlds, in these arrayed,*
> *With joy shall I lift up my head.*[6]

Not only will that be true in the future, when we ourselves come to stand before God's throne in the righteousness of Christ, but it is true now, as our prayers come to him and are received into sovereign hands with love and care and joy. What an encouragement to come to God in the name of and through faith in the Lord Jesus Christ. To him be glory forever.

241

NOTES

PREFACE

1. D. Martyn Lloyd-Jones, *God's Ultimate Purpose: An Exposition of Ephesians 1* (Grand Rapids: Baker, 1978), 6.

CHAPTER 1: GRACE AND PEACE TO YOU

1. See P. T. O'Brien, *The Letter to the Ephesians* (Grand Rapids: Eerdmans, 1999), 1.

2. See John R. W. Stott, *The Message of Ephesians* (Downers Grove, Ill.: InterVarsity Press, 1979), 15–16.

3. James Montgomery Boice, *Ephesians* (Grand Rapids: Zondervan, 1988), 11.

4. F. F. Bruce, *Paul: Apostle of the Heart Set Free* (Grand Rapids: Eerdmans, 1977), 15–16.

5. Thomas R. Schreiner, *Paul: Apostle of God's Glory in Christ* (Downers Grove, Ill.: InterVarsity Press, 2001), 37–38.

6. D. Martyn Lloyd-Jones, *Romans: The Gospel of God, An Exposition of Romans 1* (Carlisle, Pa.: Banner of Truth, 1985), 38.

7. O'Brien, *The Letter to the Ephesians*, 84.

8. William Barclay, *The Letters to the Galatians and Ephesians* (Philadelphia: Westminster, 1976), 64.

9. Charles Hodge, *A Commentary on Ephesians* (Carlisle, Pa.: Banner of Truth, 1964), xii.

10. For a thorough critique of the argument against Pauline authorship, see O'Brien, *The Letter to the Ephesians*, 4–46.

11. D. Martyn Lloyd-Jones, *God's Ultimate Purpose: An Exposition of Ephesians 1* (Grand Rapids: Baker, 1978), 36.

12. Leon Morris, *Expository Reflections on the Letter to the Ephesians* (Grand Rapids: Baker, 1994), 13.

13. R. C. Sproul: *The Mystery of the Holy Spirit* (Wheaton, Ill.: Tyndale, 1990), 170–71.

14. Lloyd-Jones, *God's Ultimate Purpose,* 38.

15. Boice, *Ephesians,* 111–12.

CHAPTER 2: WHAT IS A CHRISTIAN?

1. See John Armstrong, *Five Great Evangelists* (Ross-shire, UK: Christian Focus, 1997), 88–93.

2. Catechism of the Catholic Church (New York: Doubleday, 1995), 828.

3. Ibid., 2683.

4. Ibid., 2156.

5. Ibid., 956.

6. H. A. Ironside, *Letters to a Roman Catholic Priest* (Neptune, N.J.: Loizeaux Brothers, 1914), 26.

7. Leon Morris, *Expository Reflections on the Letter to the Ephesians* (Grand Rapids: Baker, 1994), 11.

8. D. Martyn Lloyd-Jones, *God's Ultimate Purpose: An Exposition of Ephesians 1* (Grand Rapids: Baker, 1978), 27.

9. See Ravi Zacharias: *Can Man Live Without God?* (Dallas: Word, 1994), 94.

10. Augustus M. Toplady.

CHAPTER 3: BLESSING FOR BLESSING

1. Alexander Maclaren, *Expositions of Holy Scripture,* 18 vols. (Grand Rapids: Baker, 1982), 13:9.

2. E. Norden; see P. T. O'Brien, *The Letter to the Ephesians* (Grand Rapids: Eerdmans, 1999), 90.

3. See Leon Morris: *Expository Reflections on the Letter to the Ephesians* (Grand Rapids: Baker, 1994), 13.

4. B. B. Warfield, *Faith and Life* (Carlisle, Pa.: Banner of Truth, 1974), 262.

5. Hugh Martin, *Christ for Us* (Carlisle, Pa.: Banner of Truth, 1998), 210.

6. Ibid., 212–13.

7. John R. W. Stott, *The Message of Ephesians* (Downers Grove, Ill.: Inter-Varsity Press, 1979), 35.

8. Martin, *Christ for Us,* 216, 219.

CHAPTER 4: CHOSEN IN CHRIST

1. John Calvin, *The Mystery of Godliness* (Morgan, Pa.: Soli Deo Gloria, 1999), 11.

2. See A. A. Hodge, *The Confession of Faith* (Carlisle, Pa.: Banner of Truth, 1958), 127, and Herman Witsius, *The Economy of the Covenants Between God and Man,* 2 vols. (Phillipsburg, N.J.: P&R, 1990), 1:171.

3. Arthur W. Pink, *The Sovereignty of God* (1918; Grand Rapids: Baker, 1984), 218, 219.

4. D. Martyn Lloyd-Jones, *God's Ultimate Purpose: An Exposition of Ephesians 1* (Grand Rapids: Baker, 1978), 103–4.

5. B. B. Warfield: *The Savior of the World* (Carlisle, Pa.: Banner of Truth, 1991), 239, 240.

6. Charles Haddon Spurgeon, *Songs in the Night,* from *Spurgeon's Sermons,* 10 vols. (Grand Rapids: Baker, 1883), 2:173–74.

7. Calvin, *The Mystery of Godliness,* 87.

8. James Montgomery Boice, "Alive in Christ," in *Hymns for a Modern Reformation* (Philadelphia: Tenth Presbyterian Church, 2000), 25.

CHAPTER 5: PREDESTINED AS SONS

1. J. I. Packer: *Knowing God* (Downers Grove, Ill.: InterVarsity Press, 1979), 250.

2. John Owen, *The Glory of Christ* (Carlisle, Pa.: Banner of Truth, 1994), 50–51.

3. James Montgomery Boice, *Amazing Grace* (Wheaton, Ill.: Tyndale, 1993), 56.

4. Jonathan Edwards, *The Works of Jonathan Edwards,* 2 vols. (Edinburgh and Carlisle, Pa.: Banner of Truth, 1976), 2:853.

5. A. W. Tozer, *The Tozer Pulpit,* book 1, *Selections from His Pulpit Ministry* (Camp Hill, Pa.: Christian Publications, 1994), 89.

6. John Newton, "Amazing Grace."

7. James Montgomery Boice, *Ephesians* (Grand Rapids: Zondervan, 1988), 25.

8. Sinclair B. Ferguson, *Children of the Living God* (Edinburgh and Carlisle, Pa.: Banner of Truth, 1989), 36–38.

9. Eric J. Alexander, "My Gracious Lord, Your Love Is Vast" (Philadelphia, 2001).

CHAPTER 6: THE GLORY OF HIS GRACE

1. John Calvin, *Calvin's New Testament Commentaries,* trans. T. H. L. Parker, 12 vols. (Grand Rapids: Eerdmans, 1965), 11:127.

2. H. A. Ironside, *Ephesians* (Neptune, N.J.: Loizeaux Brothers, 2000), 33–34.

3. Ibid., 36.

4. John R. W. Stott, *The Message of Ephesians* (Downers Grove, Ill.: InterVarsity Press, 1979), 39.

5. Ironside, *Ephesians,* 35.

6. "When I Survey the Wondrous Cross."

CHAPTER 7: REDEMPTION IN CHRIST

1. D. Martyn Lloyd-Jones, *God's Ultimate Purpose: An Exposition of Ephesians 1* (Grand Rapids: Baker, 1978), 148.

2. Charles Wesley, "O for a Thousand Tongues to Sing."

3. Matthew Bridges, "Crown Him with Many Crowns."

4. Philip P. Bliss, "I Will Sing of My Redeemer."

5. James Montgomery Boice, *Foundations of the Christian Faith* (Downers Grove, Ill.: InterVarsity Press, 1986), 327.

6. John Murray, *Redemption Accomplished and Applied* (Grand Rapids: Eerdmans, 1955), 47.

7. Charles Colson, *Who Speaks for God?* (Wheaton, Ill.: Crossway, 1985), 76–77.

8. Charles Hodge, *A Commentary on Ephesians* (Carlisle, Pa.: Banner of Truth, 1964), 17.

9. R. Kent Hughes, *Ephesians: The Mystery of the Body of Christ* (Wheaton, Ill.: Crossway, 1990), 35.

10. Horatius Bonar, "Not What My Hands Have Done."

11. Boice, *Foundations of the Christian Faith,* 329–30.

12. Horatius Bonar, "Not What My Hands Have Done."

CHAPTER 8: THE BLOOD OF CHRIST

1. John R. W. Stott, *The Cross of Christ* (Downers Grove, Ill.: InterVarsity Press, 1986), 19–20.

2. Ibid., 23.

3. See ibid., 24.

4. Sir Alfred Ayer; see John R. W. Stott, *The Message of Ephesians* (Downers Grove, Ill.: InterVarsity Press, 1979), 43.

5. See ibid., 42.

6. J. I. Packer: *Knowing God* (Downers Grove, Ill.: InterVarsity Press, 1978), 136.

7. William Cowper, "There Is a Fountain."

8. Count Nikolaus Ludwig von Zinzendorf, trans. John Wesley, "Jesus, Thy Blood and Righteousness."

9. While I cannot cite a specific reference, I am indebted to R. C. Sproul for the formulation "saved from God, to God, by God." I have heard him articulate this formula in addresses on a number of occasions, and I am sure it occurs in at least one of his books.

10. Charles Wesley, "And Can It Be."

11. John Shelby Spong, *Why Christianity Must Change or Die* (San Francisco: HarperCollins, 1999), 95.

12. Ibid., 83.

13. George Bennard, "Old Rugged Cross."

14. Robert Lowry, "Nothing but the Blood."

15. See Stott, *The Cross of Christ*, 43.

16. D. Martyn Lloyd-Jones, *The Heart of the Gospel* (Wheaton, Ill.: Crossway, 1991), 33.

CHAPTER 9: THE SALVATION MYSTERY

1. See William Barclay, *The Letters to the Galatians and Ephesians* (Philadelphia: Westminster, 1976), 85.

2. P. T. O'Brien, *The Letter to the Ephesians* (Grand Rapids: Eerdmans, 1999), 111–12.

3. Charles Hodge, *A Commentary on Ephesians* (Carlisle, Pa.: Banner of Truth, 1964), 27.

4. John Bunyan, *Pilgrim's Progress* (Nashville: Thomas Nelson, 1999), 134–37.

CHAPTER 10: THE GLORIOUS PLAN OF GOD

1. G. Campbell Morgan, *The Westminster Pulpit*, 10 vols. (Grand Rapids: Baker, 1995), 1:48.

2. D. Martyn Lloyd-Jones, *Saved in Eternity* (Wheaton, Ill.: Crossway, 1988), 48.

3. C. S. Lewis: *The Weight of Glory and Other Addresses* (New York: Macmillan, 1975), 8.

4. Charles Hodge, *A Commentary on Ephesians* (Carlisle, Pa.: Banner of Truth, 1964), 32–33.

5. James Montgomery Boice, *Ephesians* (Grand Rapids: Zondervan, 1988), 34–35.

6. John Calvin, *Sermons on the Epistle to the Ephesians* (Carlisle, Pa.: Banner of Truth, 1973), 47.

7. John R. W. Stott, *The Message of Ephesians* (Downers Grove, Ill.: InterVarsity Press, 1979), 50.

8. See James Montgomery Boice, *The Minor Prophets*, 2 vols. (Grand Rapids: Zondervan, 1983), 1:23.

CHAPTER 11: MARKED WITH A SEAL

1. John Bunyan, *The Pilgrim's Progress* (Nashville: Thomas Nelson, 1999), 136.

2. Charles Hodge, *A Commentary on Ephesians* (Carlisle, Pa.: Banner of Truth, 1964), 32.

3. Leon Morris, *Expository Reflections on the Letter to the Ephesians* (Grand Rapids: Baker, 1994), 26.

4. Hodge, *A Commentary on Ephesians,* 35.

5. Jonathan Edwards, *The Distinguishing Marks of a Work of the Spirit of God,* in *Jonathan Edwards on Revival* (Carlisle, Pa.: Banner of Truth, 1965), 91.

6. Ibid., 115.

7. John Calvin, *Sermons on the Epistle to the Ephesians* (Carlisle, Pa.: Banner of Truth, 1973), 72.

8. Ibid., 73.

9. Bunyan, *Pilgrim's Progress,* 35–36.

CHAPTER 12: THE DEPOSIT OF OUR INHERITANCE

1. James R. White, *The Forgotten Trinity* (Minneapolis: Bethany House, 1998), 16.

2. Ibid., 13.

3. Robert Reymond, *A New Systematic Theology of the Christian Faith* (Nashville: Thomas Nelson, 1998), 763–64.

4. Handley C. G. Moule, *The Person and Work of the Holy Spirit* (Grand Rapids: Kregel, 1977), 11–12.

5. Geoffrey B. Wilson, *Ephesians* (Carlisle, Pa.: Banner of Truth, 1978), 32.

6. Donald Grey Barnhouse, *Expositions of Bible Doctrines Taking the Epistle to the Romans as a Point of Departure,* 10 vols. (Grand Rapids: Eerdmans, 1959), 4:140.

7. John Grisham, *The Testament* (New York: Doubleday, 1999).

8. John Owen, *Communion with God* (Carlisle, Pa.: Banner of Truth, 1991), 186–87.

9. R. Kent Hughes, *Ephesians: The Mystery of the Body of Christ* (Wheaton, Ill.: Crossway, 1990), 46.

CHAPTER 13: PAUL'S PRAYER FOR THE CHURCH

1. Arthur W. Pink, *The Ability of God* (Chicago: Moody Press, 2000), 13.

2. Jeremiah Burroughs, *Gospel Worship* (Morgan, Pa.: Soli Deo Gloria, 1990), 55–56.

3. Dietrich Bonhoeffer, *Life Together* (San Francisco: Harper & Row, 1954), 86.

4. Pink, *The Ability of God,* 15.

5. D. A. Carson, *A Call to Spiritual Reformation* (Grand Rapids: Baker, 1992), 170.

6. James Montgomery Boice, *Romans,* vol. 1, *Justification by Faith* (Grand Rapids: Baker, 1991), 76.

7. William Edgar, "United in Love," in *The Communion of the Saints*, ed. Philip Ryken (Phillipsburg, N.J.: P&R, 2001), 57–58.

8. Richard Sibbes, *Works*, 6 vols. (reprint, Edinburgh: Banner of Truth, 1979–83), 3:433.

9. Francis A. Schaeffer, *The Mark of the Christian* (Downers Grove, Ill.: InterVarsity Press, 1970), 17–18.

10. James Montgomery Boice, *Ephesians* (Grand Rapids: Zondervan, 1988), 41.

11. E. Schuyler English, *H. A. Ironside: Ordained of the Lord* (Neptune, N.J.: Loizeaux Brothers, 1976), 94.

Chapter 14: Knowing God

1. John Calvin, *Institutes of the Christian Religion*, trans. Ford Lewis Battles, 2 vols. (Philadelphia: Westminster, 1960), 1.5.1.

2. D. A. Carson, *A Call to Spiritual Reformation* (Grand Rapids: Baker, 1992), 15–16.

3. Charles Haddon Spurgeon: *The New Park Street Pulpit*, vol. 1 (1855; Pasadena, Tex.: Pilgrim Publications, 1975), 1.

4. Bruce Ware, *God's Lesser Glory: The Diminished God of Open Theism* (Wheaton, Ill.: Crossway, 2002), 21.

5. Ibid., 25–26.

6. F. F. Bruce, *The Epistles to the Colossians, to Philemon and to the Ephesians* (Grand Rapids: Eerdmans, 1984), 269.

7. Augustine, *A Treatise on the Merits and Forgiveness of Sins, and on the Baptism of Infants*, from *A Select Library of the Nicene and Post-Nicene Fathers of the Christian Church*, ed. Philip Schaff, vol. 5, *Saint Augustine: Anti-Pelagian Writings* (Peabody, Mass.: Hendrickson, 1999), 29.

8. James H. Sammis, "Trust and Obey."

Chapter 15: The Three "Whats"

1. Charles Haddon Spurgeon, *Metropolitan Tabernacle Pulpit*, 63 vols. (Pasadena, Tex.: Pilgrim Publications, 1969), 25:244.

2. Thomas Watson: *A Body of Divinity*, (Carlisle, Pa.: Banner of Truth, 1958), 296–97.

3. D. Martyn Lloyd-Jones, *God's Ultimate Purpose: An Exposition of Ephesians 1* (Grand Rapids: Baker, 1979), 324.

4. John Chrysostom, *Homilies on Ephesians*, from *Nicene and Post-Nicene Fathers, First Series*, ed. Philip Schaff, 14 vols. (Peabody, Mass.: Hendrickson, 1999), 13:61.

5. D. A. Carson, *A Call to Spiritual Reformation* (Grand Rapids: Baker, 1992), 177.

6. Leon Morris, *Expository Reflections on the Letter to the Ephesians* (Grand Rapids: Baker, 1994), 33.

7. "Come, We That Love the Lord."

CHAPTER 16: CHRIST EXALTED

1. D. Martyn Lloyd-Jones, *God's Ultimate Purpose: An Exposition of Ephesians 1* (Grand Rapids: Baker, 1978), 430.

2. Andrew T. Lincoln, *Ephesians* (Dallas: Word, 1990), 75.

3. Charles Hodge, *A Commentary on Ephesians* (Carlisle, Pa.: Banner of Truth, 1964), 54.

4. John Calvin, *The Epistles of Paul the Apostle to the Galatians, Ephesians, Philippians and Colossians* (Grand Rapids: Eerdmans, 1965), 138.

5. Arthur W. Pink, *The Ability of God* (Chicago: Moody Press, 2000), 217.

6. D. A. Carson, *A Call to Spiritual Reformation* (Grand Rapids: Baker, 1992), 179–80.

CHAPTER 17: PRAYER AND THE SOVEREIGNTY OF GOD

1. C. Samuel Storms, "Prayer and Evangelism Under God's Sovereignty," in *Still Sovereign: Contemporary Perspectives on Election, Foreknowledge, and Grace,* ed. Thomas R. Schreiner and Bruce A. Ware (Grand Rapids: Baker, 2000), 320.

2. James Montgomery Boice, *Whatever Happened to the Gospel of Grace?* (Wheaton, Ill.: Crossway, 2001), 167; see also 178.

3. See Arthur W. Pink, *The Sovereignty of God* (Grand Rapids: Baker, 1993), 168.

4. See ibid., 169.

5. Storms, "Prayer and Evangelism Under God's Sovereignty," 320.

6. Count Nikolaus Ludwig von Zinzendorf, trans. John Wesley, "Jesus, Thy Blood and Righteousness."

INDEX OF SCRIPTURE

Index of Subjects
and Names

261

Richard D. Phillips (B.A., University of Michigan; M.B.A., University of Pennsylvania; M.Div., Westminster Theological Seminary) is senior minister of First Presbyterian Church in Coral Springs/Margate, Florida. He is also speaker-at-large for the Alliance of Confessing Evangelicals and director of the Philadelphia Conference on Reformation Theology.

An officer in the United States Army for thirteen years, Phillips commanded various tank and armored cavalry units and served as assistant professor of leadership at the United States Military Academy, West Point, before resigning with the rank of major.

He is the author of *Mighty to Save, Encounters with Jesus, Faith Victorious,* and *Turning Your World Upside Down.* He lives in South Florida with his wife, Sharon, and their four children, Hannah, Matthew, Jonathan, and Helen.